W9-BNG-511

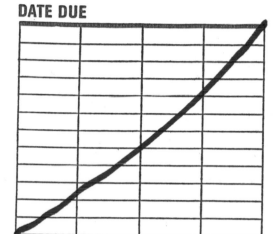

DATA ANALYSIS
FOR POLITICS
AND POLICY

DATA ANALYSIS FOR POLITICS AND POLICY

EDWARD R. TUFTE

Princeton University

PRENTICE-HALL, INC., Englewood Cliffs, N.J.

Library of Congress Cataloging in Publication Data

TUFTE, EDWARD R
    Data analysis for politics and policy.

    (Foundations of modern political science series)
    Includes bibliographical references.
    1. Social sciences—Statistical methods. 2. Polit-
ical statistics. I. Title.
HA29.T782   519.5′02′432   74-9504
ISBN 0-13-197541-2
ISBN 0-13-197525-0 (pbk.)

FOUNDATIONS OF MODERN POLITICAL SCIENCE SERIES
Editor, ROBERT A. DAHL

Printed in the United States of America
  10 9 8 7 6 5 4 3 2 1

PRENTICE-HALL INTERNATIONAL, INC., *London*
PRENTICE-HALL OF AUSTRALIA, PTY. LTD., *Sydney*
PRENTICE-HALL OF CANADA, LTD., *Toronto*
PRENTICE-HALL OF INDIA PRIVATE LIMITED, *New Delhi*
PRENTICE-HALL OF JAPAN, INC., *Tokyo*

Contents

CHAPTER **3**

TWO-VARIABLE LINEAR REGRESSION   **65**

Preface

This book demonstrates some statistical techniques useful in the study of politics and policy. My aim is to present fundamental material not found in statistics books, and, in particular, to show techniques of quantitative analysis in action on problems of politics and public policy. Most of the examples can be understood without a mathematical or statistical background; some sections require familiarity with basic statistical inference. Not all methodological bases are touched; still, in the chapters that follow, quite a number of important statistical concepts are illustrated.

The approach centers on fitting equations to data. More fundamental, however, is the illustration and development of good statistical thinking—a sense of judgment about what we can and can't learn about the world by looking at quantitative data.

Much of this material was first prepared for courses I have taught at Princeton University. I am indebted to several of my students and colleagues for suggesting improvements and also to Marver Bernstein who first encouraged me to teach a course in the quantitative analysis of public policy issues. I am deeply grateful to many people for their help, both direct and indirect, in the writing of this volume. In particular, John McCarthy read several drafts with great care; and Walter Gilbert, Walter Murphy, Dennis Thompson, and David Wallace commented on various sections of the manuscript. Over the years, Robert Dahl, Stanley Kelley, Jr., Frederick Mosteller, and John

ix

Tukey have given me good advice and encouragement on this project. Joseph G. Verbalis, Alice Anne Navin, Jan Juran, and Marge Cruise helped to gather and analyze much of the data. Mrs. Virginia Anderson prepared the final manuscript with care and accuracy. Barbra and Irma Kay Power provided a room of my own in London for writing the first draft. The section in Chapter 2 on bellwether electoral districts was coauthored with Richard A. Sun—and, without his energy and persistence, that difficult project would never have been completed. At Princeton University, the Computer Center, the Woodrow Wilson School, and the Department of Politics all provided superb institutional support. Finally, a fellowship at the Center for Advanced Study in the Behavioral Sciences in 1973–74 gave me time for final revisions. These individuals and institutions are not, of course, responsible for the faults of the book; they did help me very much and I am deeply indebted to them.

E. R. T.

THE FAIRLY INTELLIGENT FLY*

A large spider in an old house built a beautiful web in which to catch flies. Every time a fly landed on the web and was entangled in it the spider devoured him, so that when another fly came along he would think the web was a safe and quiet place in which to rest. One day a fairly intelligent fly buzzed around above the web so long without lighting that the spider appeared and said, "Come on down." But the fly was too clever for him and said, "I never light where I don't see other flies and I don't see any other flies in your house." So he flew away until he came to a place where there were a great many other flies. He was about to settle down among them when a bee buzzed up and said, "Hold it, stupid, that's flypaper. All those flies are trapped." "Don't be silly," said the fly, "they're dancing." So he settled down and became stuck to the flypaper with all the other flies.

Moral: There is no safety in numbers, or in anything else.

James Thurber,
Fables for Our Time

*Reproduced from *Fables for Our Time* by James Thurber. Copyright © 1940 by James Thurber; © 1968 by Helen Thurber. Published by Harper & Row, Publishers, New York. Originally printed in *the New Yorker*. Permission for British rights by Hamish Hamilton, Ltd.

CHAPTER 1

Introduction to Data Analysis

"Because that's where they keep the money."

—Willie Sutton, *when asked why he robbed banks*

Introduction

Students of political and social problems use statistical techniques to help

test theories and explanations by confronting them with empirical evidence,

summarize a large body of data into a small collection of typical values,

confirm that relationships in the data did not arise merely because of happenstance or random error,

discover some new relationship in the data, and

inform readers about what is going on in the data.

The use of statistical methods to analyze data does not make a study any more "scientific," "rigorous," or "objective." The purpose of quantitative analysis is not to sanctify a set of findings. Unfortunately, some studies, in the words of one critic, "use statistics as a drunk uses a street lamp, for support rather than illumination." Quantitative techniques will be more likely to illuminate if the data analyst is guided in methodological choices by a substantive understanding of the problem he or she is trying to learn about. Good procedures in data analysis involve techniques that help to (a) answer the substantive questions at hand, (b) squeeze all the relevant information out of the data, and (c) learn something new about the world.

Causal Explanation

All inquiry begins with a problem, a question to be answered. Why have some countries, despite great natural resources, remained economically weak? Why do some nations spend more on military equipment than others? Does smoking cause lung cancer? Do automobile safety inspections reduce the number of traffic accidents? Do economic conditions help determine what candidates the people vote for?

The thing to be explained is the *response variable* or *dependent variable*. In the questions above, the response variables are, respectively, the level of economic development, military expenditures, the frequency of lung cancer, the number of traffic accidents, and an individual's choice in an election. The causes, explanations, or predictors of the response variable are the *describing variables* or *independent variables*. Usually more than one describing variable will help explain the response variable; and an analysis with several describing variables is called, in the jargon, *multivariate analysis*. For example, two causes of lung cancer might be smoking and amount of time spent in a coal mine. Here the two describing variables are the amount of smoking and amount of time digging coal (and inhaling coal and rock dust).

Although it is sometimes difficult to speak in causal terms in studies of social problems, it is clear that if we want to explain or change anything, we will eventually have to work in terms of cause and effect. As Dahl put it, "policy-thinking is and must be causality-thinking."[1] Wold has even suggested a link between explanation and policy outcomes:

> A frequent situation is that description serves to maintain some *modus vivendi* (the control of an established production process, the tolerance of a limited number of epidemic cases), whereas explanation serves the purpose of *reform* (raising the agricultural yield, reducing the mortality rates, improving a production process). In other words, description is employed as an aid in the human *adjustment* to conditions, while explanation is a vehicle for ascendancy over the environment.[2]

[1] Robert A. Dahl, "Cause and Effect in the Study of Politics," in Daniel Lerner, ed., *Cause and Effect* (New York: Free Press, 1965), p. 88

[2] Herman Wold, "Causal Inference from Observational Data," *Journal of the Royal Statistical Society*, Series A, 119 (1956), p. 29.

Sometimes, especially in studies based on data collected from observational records rather than from controlled experiments, researchers avoid causal language and use wishy-washy phrases to report their results: one variable is said to "predict" another: or a variable is "strongly related," "associated," or "varies regularly" with another variable. The language of association and prediction is probably most often used because the evidence seems insufficient to justify a direct causal statement. A better practice is to state the causal hypothesis and then to present the evidence along with an assessment with respect to the causal hypothesis—instead of letting the quality of the data determine the language of the explanation.

In other cases, researchers appear only interested in studying associations and have no causal mechanisms in mind. These studies seek to discover "patterns of association" and "clusters of interrelated variables." Such discoveries can sometimes be a helpful first step toward developing explanations.

A good research design is a successful strategy for collecting and analyzing data that help to assess the validity of competing explanations of the variation in the response variable. In causal analysis, the basic purpose of research design is to observe or control covariation between the response and describing variables in a context such that these variables are not confounded with other uncontrolled or extraneous influences. Thus the key element in developing and testing explanations is *controlled comparison.* By such comparison we evaluate and decide among theories about what variables cause what effects. The importance of comparison or control groups in making inferences is illustrated by Cochran's account of a study by Seltser and Sartwell on the effects of exposure to atomic radiation:

> As pointed out by Seltser and Sartwell, the principal opportunities for investigations in human subjects are confined to the following: (a) the Japanese survivors of the atomic bombs in Hiroshima and Nagasaki, involving a single exposure, (b) groups occupationally exposed to radiation at times when the possible danger from this source was not realized—radiologists, dentists, and makers of watches with luminous dials, (c) persons who received medical radiation, as in the treatment of some forms of cancer, or infants exposed *in utero* through pelvic X-rays of the mother in the late stages of pregnancy, and (d) areas of the earth in which natural radioactivity is unusually high.
>
> None of these sources provides more than limited material for constructing a dosage-response curve. . . .
>
> The study by Seltser and Sartwell of the mortality of radiologists is an excellent example of the possibilities from groups occupationally or medically exposed. They chose male members of the Radiological Society of North America. For each member they obtained by a

painstaking search the status (dead or alive) as of December 31, 1958, with cause of death and any available information on other factors such as age that might influence duration of life. *Research of this type always raises the question: with what are the exposed group to be compared? Ideally, we seek a non-exposed group which is similar to the exposed group with regard to any other variable that is known or suspected to have a material effect on duration of life. . . . In an observational study the extent to which this goal can be met is of course dependent on our ability to measure such variables and to find a group that has similar distributions with respect to them.*

The authors chose two comparison groups. As the nearest to a non-exposed group they used the American Academy of Opthalmology and Otolaryngology, whose members rarely have occasion to employ X-radiation. As an intermediate group they also included the American College of Physicians, since some of these members use X-rays, for example, in ear examinations. In such studies the inclusion of a middle group is advantageous in either adding confirmation to the results given by the two extreme groups or in casting doubt upon them. This study, however, again has the weakness that no measures of the doses of radiation experienced by the subjects are available, except as a rough guess for the group as a whole. Studies similar in structure have been done of the later development of infants *in utero*, as compared with a control group of non-exposed infants born in the same hospital at the same time.[3]

The importance of controlled comparison in the assessment of causal relationships is made even more bluntly in a doctor's story about the evaluation of surgical procedures:

One day when I was a junior medical student, a very important Boston surgeon visited the school and delivered a great treatise on a large number of patients who had undergone successful operation for vascular reconstruction. At the end of the lecture, a young student at the back of the room timidly asked, "Do you have any controls?" Well, the great surgeon drew himself up to his full height, hit the desk, and said, "Do you mean did I not operate on half of the patients?" The hall grew very quiet then. The voice at the back of the room very hesitantly replied, "Yes, that's what I had in mind." Then the visitor's fist really came down as he thundered, "Of course not. That would have doomed half of them to their death." God, it was quiet then, and one could scarcely hear the small voice ask, "Which half?"[4]

---

[3]William G. Cochran, "Planning and Analysis of Non-Experimental Studies," ONR Technical Report No. 19 (April 1968), Department of Statistics, Harvard University, pp. 7–9, italics added. The cited study is R. Seltser and P. E. Sartwell, "The Influence of Occupational Exposure to Radiation on the Mortality of American Radiologists and Other Medical Specialists," *American Journal of Epidemiology*, 81 (1965), 2–22.

[4]Dr. E. E. Peacock, Jr., Chairman of Surgery, University of Arizona College of Medicine; quoted in *Medical World News* (September 1, 1972), p. 45. I am indebted to my colleague Herman Somers for pointing out this citation to me.

One final point about the relationship between causal inferences and statistical analysis. Statistical techniques do not solve any of the common-sense difficulties about making causal inferences. Such techniques may help organize or arrange the data so that the numbers speak more clearly to the question of causality—but that is all statistical techniques can do. All the logical, theoretical, and empirical difficulties attendant to establishing a causal relationship persist no matter what type of statistical analysis is applied. "There is," as Thurber moralized, "no safety in numbers, or in anything else."

An Example: Do Automobile Safety Inspections Save Lives?

Let us now go through an example, analyzing some data to answer a particular question and, in the process, showing several basic techniques for looking at a collection of data. We will, in this example, try to find out whether compulsory automobile safety inspections (the describing variable) help reduce traffic fatalities (the response variable).

In 1967, nineteen states in the United States had some form of automobile safety inspection with the consequent correction of mechanical defects. Some states, such as New Jersey, had rather thorough yearly inspections, testing headlight alignment, other lights, brakes, steering, and tires. Other states had superficial inspections; most had none at all.

Inspections can produce significant benefits if they help to reduce the yearly toll of 55,000 deaths and 4.4 million minor and major injuries resulting from automobile crashes. The economic costs, too, are considerable: "A disproportionate number of the persons killed or permanently disabled represents an almost complete loss on a heavy investment: they are persons with twenty years of nurture behind them and presumedly forty years of productive work ahead. The cost estimates are surpassingly fuzzy, but something like 2 percent of the Gross National Product seems about right, if property damage accidents are included."[5] Finally, one estimate is that "perhaps 20 percent of the automobile industry is required to replace or repair damaged vehicles."[6]

But inspections also have significant costs, both of administration and enforcement as well as of delay and aggravation to the individual driver, who must often spend several hours having his car examined.

[5] Daniel P. Moynihan, "The War Against the Automobile," *The Public Interest*, no. 3 (Spring 1966), p. 10.
[6] *Ibid.*, p. 13

Inspections cost directly about $500 million each year—plus the hidden and nonfinancial costs to the individual driver. There are good reasons, then, for trying to find out whether inspections make any difference. If they do actually reduce the death rate significantly, inspection programs should be strengthened; if they have little effect, then the money might be better spent some other way.

We can imagine a controlled experiment—first choosing randomly a large number of cars, inspecting them and correcting their mechanical defects, and then following their history of accidents for several years. Another group of cars, remaining uninspected, would serve as a comparison or control group. Such an experiment would require a rather large sample, since fatal auto crashes are a relatively rare event, with about one car in a thousand being involved in a fatal accident in a given year. (Many cars during their lifetime, however, are in some sort of accident and probably at least one car in three winds up with blood on it.[7])

Not only would the sample have to be large, but it would have to be randomly chosen. We couldn't rely entirely on volunteers, because those car owners who volunteered to have their cars inspected and to participate in the experiment would be likely to be quite different from the typical car owner. The more safety-conscious driver who owned a car with few mechanical defects would probably be more likely to volunteer than the owner of a dilapidated car. And so we would have to take steps to avoid a bias toward safety-conscious drivers, for they would probably be overrepresented in a volunteer group and other types of drivers underrepresented.

Unfortunately, few such social experiments of this type have ever been tried. Donald T. Campbell points out in his paper "Reforms as Experiments" that "The United States and other modern nations should be ready for an experimental approach to social reform, an approach in which we try out new programs designed to cure specific social problems, in which we learn whether or not these programs are effective, and in which we retain, imitate, modify or discard them on the basis of apparent effectiveness. . . . [M]ost ameliorative programs end up with *no* interpretable evaluation."[8]

What are some alternatives to a large-scale experiment—which would be the most inferentially sound way to study the problem—in order to evaluate the impact, if any, of automobile inspections? Two other methods provide help. First, a *time-series analysis* follows the trend of the death rate before and then after the adoption of inspections

[7] *Ibid.*
[8] *American Psychologist,* 24 (1969), p. 409.

in a given state. In other words, for each of the states that now have inspections, the job is to see whether fatalities decreased after the inspections were started. The states that still do not have inspections can be used as a comparison or control group to test other explanations (other than introduction of inspections) for changes in the death rate over time. Thus the control group helps us find out whether the fatality rate goes down, relative to similar states, when inspections are introduced in a given state.[9]

The second method, a *cross-section analysis*, compares at a given point in time the death rates in those states that have inspections with the death rates in those states without inspections. The important assumption here is that other factors affecting the death rate are equal for the inspected and the uninspected states. "Other things being equal" is sometimes only a faint hope, although often we can insure that at least some important things are approximately equal.

The remainder of this chapter consists of a cross-section analysis of the effects of inspections. The purpose is to show some basic concepts of data analysis by means of a substantive example. In the cross-section approach, the question becomes: "Do states that have automobile safety inspections have lower fatality rates than those states without inspections—other things being equal?" Comparing the variations in rates between inspected and uninspected states is not a perfect test—partly because both inspected and uninspected cars can cross state lines and be involved in accidents in other states. Furthermore, inspections may constitute part of a larger safety program that includes strong checks on drunken driving, better roads, and so forth. Thus, it might be more appropriate to attribute differences in death rates to an overall safety program in the state rather than just to inspections.

In summary, even if rates are low in inspected compared to uninspected states, we want to be very careful in attributing variations in rates only to the presence or absence of inspections. These and other complicating factors work against getting a clean test of the relationship between inspections and death rates. Such confounding factors enter into almost every analysis of social and political problems.

(WARNING: Typically, data analysis is messy, and little details clutter it. Not only confounding factors, but also deviant cases, minor problems in measurement, and ambiguous results lead to frustration and discouragement, so that more data are collected than analyzed. Ne-

[9] A good example of such a study is Donald T. Campbell and H. Laurence Ross, "The Connecticut Crackdown on Speeding: Time-Series Data in Quasi-Experimental Analysis," *Law and Society Review*, 3 (August 1968), 33–53, and reprinted in Edward R. Tufte, ed., *The Quantitative Analysis of Social Problems* (Reading, Mass.: Addison-Wesley, 1970) pp. 110–25.

glecting or hiding the messy details of the data reduces the researchers chances of discovering something new. One common error is to underestimate the time necessary for the analysis. Although there is a good deal of variability, in many projects the analysis and synthesis of the data consume 80 to 90 percent of the total time spent. Often, after the initial collection and first analysis of the data, it is necessary and wise to go back and acquire additional information suggested by the first results. A good rule of thumb for deciding how long the analysis of the data actually will take is

(1) to add up all the time for *everything* you can think of—editing the data, checking for errors, calculating various statistics, thinking about the results, going back to the data to try out a new idea, and

(2) then multiply the estimate obtained in this first step by five. With these words of warning, let us get on with the present analysis).

The fifty states differ greatly in their automobile fatality rates: Connecticut, with the lowest rate, had 14.8 deaths per 100,000 residents in 1968; Wyoming, the highest, had a rate more than three times greater at 52.1 deaths per 100,000 people.[10] Figure 1-1 reveals the wide variation in death rates for the states. If all states had a death rate as low as Connecticut, instead of 55,000 deaths in automobile accidents each, only 30,000 deaths would occur—a reduction of 46 percent.

Figure 1-1, on page 10, shows a cluster of three states with rather high rates: Wyoming, Nevada, and New Mexico all have rates near 50. Three other states—Idaho, Arizona, and Montana—also are quite high with rates exceeding 40 deaths per 100,000 people per year. Six states distinguish themselves at the low end of the scale: Connecticut, Rhode Island, Massachusetts, New York, Hawaii, and New Jersey all have rates less than 20. Already, perhaps, we can see some characteristics of high-rate compared to low-rate states:

States with extremely high rates are more likely	*States with extremely low rates are more likely*
—to be located in the western part of the United States	—to be located in the eastern part of the United States
—to be thinly populated (i.e., low density, few people per square mile)	—to be thickly populated (i.e., high density, many people per square mile)
—not to have been one of the original 13 states of the United States	—to have been one of the original 13 states of the United States

[10] Accident rates, unless otherwise noted, are taken from the appropriate annual edition of *Accidents Facts* (Chicago: National Safety Council).

States with extremely high rates are more likely	States with extremely low rates are more likely
—not to have inspections	—to have inspections
—to have seven or less letters in their names	—to have more than seven letters in their names

A number of factors, of varying relevance to be sure, seem to be associated with the death rate for the extremely high and extremely low states. Note that while we observe many different associations between the death rate and other characteristics of the state, it is our substantive judgment, and not merely the observed association, that tells us density and inspections might have something to do with the death rate and that the number of letters in the name of the state has nothing to do with it.

So far we have looked only at the states with either extremely high or extremely low death rates. Such a procedure, while giving some useful indications, can also be misleading: all the data should be used, not just a fraction.

In looking at Figure 1-1, one should begin to wonder just how reliable these figures are. Perhaps Wyoming is high because a bad accident involving many deaths—such as a bus accident—occurred in 1968. In a "normal" year, would Wyoming have a lower death rate? Would a different set of states fall at the low end of the scale a year before or a year after these data were collected? Do Wyoming, New Mexico, and Nevada usually have high rates—and do Rhode Island, Connecticut, and Massachusetts usually have low rates? In short, then, how do the rates vary from year to year? These questions are good ones, because if the variation in death rates across the different states changed wildly from one year to the next, we might begin to suspect that states were merely high or low because they were "lucky" or "unlucky," because they had a few accidents resulting in many deaths in a "bad" year.

These questions are easy to answer. A number of different approaches all produce the same result: the large differences between states in their death rates have remained relatively persistent over the years. For example, the five states with the highest death rates in 1948 also had the five highest death rates in 1958 and again in 1968. Similarly the states with the five lowest death rates in 1948 were also the five lowest in 1958; in 1968, four of these five remained among the five lowest. Figure 1-2 also gives a sharp and clear answer. This scatterplot plots each state's 1958 death rate against its 1968 rate. The picture shows:

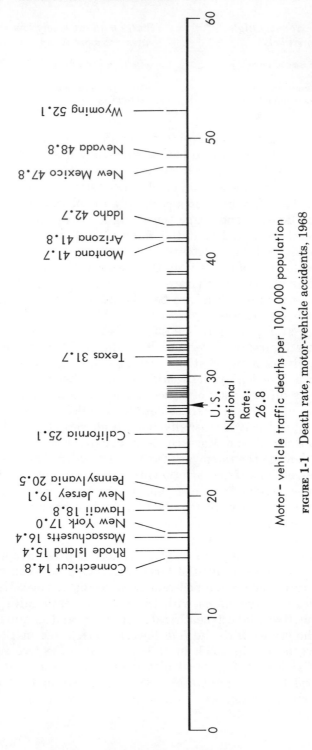

Motor-vehicle traffic deaths per 100,000 population

FIGURE 1-1   Death rate, motor-vehicle accidents, 1968

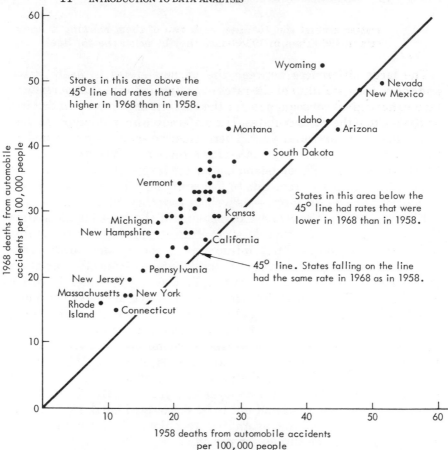

FIGURE 1-2   Death rates, 1958 and 1968

1. The states that had high rates in 1958 remained high in 1968; those with average death rates in 1958 had similar rates in 1968; and low rates in 1958 continued to be low in 1968. Such a relationship is called a positive relationship; as one variable grows bigger, so does the other variable. The scatterplot shows a fairly strong relationship in that the points increase in a relatively orderly fashion; they are not scattered all over the graph. In summary, there is a strong positive relationship between rates for 1958 and 1968.

2. Most states have somewhat higher rates in 1968 than they did ten years earlier, since most states lie *above* the 45° line (which is the area where the 1968 rate always exceeds the 1958 rate). All of the states with middle-level death rates show some increase between 1958 and 1968, since they lie above the line in the area where the 1968 rate is always greater than the 1958 rate. Finally, those states with very high death rates show a fair amount of

scatter around the 45° line, with two of them showing a lower rate in 1968 than in 1958 (since they lie *below* the 45° line).

The large differences between the various states in death rates and the relative stability of the rates over time indicate that persistent factors have great consequences for the risk one assumes when driving on the roads of the various states. The differences are not happenstance or peculiar to a particular year. There must be *something* that makes the death rate consistently three times higher in Wyoming than in Rhode Island. Since Rhode Island has safety inspections and Wyoming does not, it appears worthwhile to look into the relationship between inspections and death rates. —as well as for other relationships.

Figure 1-2 shows the relative persistence of the rates for the states; the unique yearly variation does not dramatically shuffle the states relative to one another. But influences on the accident death rate peculiar or unique to a given year do contribute to some of the variation in a single year's set of accident figures for each state. In order to reduce the effect of such influences, we will average out the unique yearly variation by averaging the death rate for each state over a three-year period—with the hope of producing a fairer picture of the typical or normal behavior of the accident rate in a state. Thus, for example, the rates for Montana in 1966, 1967, and 1968 were 39.3, 45.5, and 41.7. The middle year, 1967, was unusually high and not typical of the long-run rate over the years in Montana. Yet it is an actual piece of data and not to be discounted entirely. A useful compromise, then, is the averaging technique. For Montana, the average rate over the three-year period is

$$\frac{39.3 + 45.5 + 41.7}{3} = 42.2.$$

This procedure is repeated for the remaining 49 states to compute a three-year death rate. This average rate is the response variable, the thing we are trying to explain.

Do inspections make any difference in these death rates? Figure 1-3 reveals that states with inspections tend to have lower death rates than states without inspections, although the two groups of states overlap a good deal. Most states with inspections, as the figure shows, beat the average for the uninspected states, although one inspected state, New Mexico, has an extremely high death rate compared to the rest of the inspected states. In the states without inspections, Connecticut has a very low rate (Connecticut has inspections for used cars that are sold in the state but not for new cars).

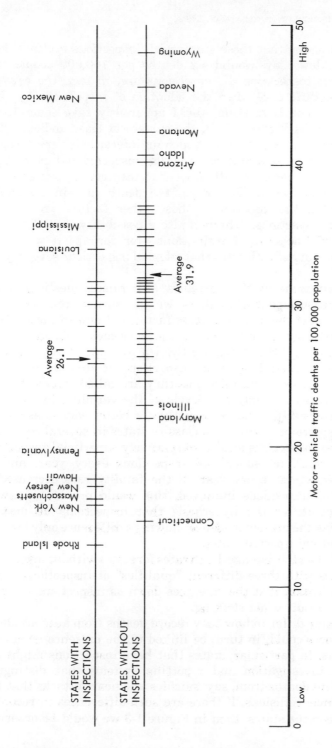

FIGURE 1-3 Inspected vs. uninspected states: averaged death rates

13

Figure 1-3 shows that those states with inspections typically have a death rate lower by around six deaths per 100,000 people than states without inspections. If inspections are, in fact, the cause of this observed difference, then the adoption of inspections by those states that do not have them would apparently save some 15,000 lives a year. Thus Figure 1-3, on the surface at least, indicates that inspections are very effective. But such an inference is very insecure. The most important source of doubt is that inspected and uninspected states may differ not only with respect to inspections, but also with respect to other factors that affect the death rate in automobile accidents. Thus the benefits of these other factors are wrongly attributed to inspections. (There is also a possibility that Figure 1-3 understates the benefits of inspections—for perhaps it was states with especially high death rates that adopted inspections several years ago.)

The measurement of the variables also raises questions. After discussing measurement difficulties, we will turn to the even more serious problem of the impact of other factors not now in the analysis.

1. The describing variable, inspections, is not measured particularly well. Right now, all the states are thrown into one of two mutually exclusive bins: either they have inspections or they do not. Such *dichotomous* or *dummy* variables, as they are called, should be used when there really are only two levels of the variable. In this case, since inspections differ widely in quality, a better way to assess the effects of inspections would be to classify states in several categories such as (a) no inspections at all, (b) relatively superficial inspections every other year, (c) superficial inspections every year, and (d) extensive inspections every year. If the fatality rate decreased as the quality of inspections improved, this would provide somewhat stronger support for the hypothesis that inspections do make a difference than the present evidence showing a difference only between inspected and uninspected states.

Figure 1-4 plots the average death rates for states without inspections and for states with three different "qualities" of inspections. There is a mild indication that the rate goes down as inspections improve, although the result is not striking.

2. States may differ in how they record deaths from auto accidents; such differences could, in turn, be linked to the presence or absence of inspections. In particular, states that have inspections might also have better investigation and reporting systems that distinguish traffic-accident deaths from, say, suicides and heart attacks that lead to motor-vehicle collisions. If there are such differences in recording deaths between the states, then in Figure 1-3 we would be observing

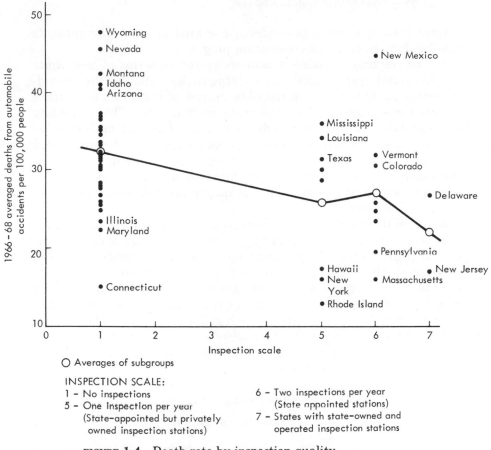

FIGURE 1-4 Death rate by inspection quality

○ Averages of subgroups

INSPECTION SCALE:
1 – No inspections
5 – One Inspection per year
    (State-appointed but privately
    owned inspection stations)

6 – Two inspections per year
    (State appointed stations)
7 – States with state–owned and
    operated inspection stations

a difference due to reporting of deaths rather than to inspections.

In such situations it is not enough to say: "There's error in the data and therefore the study must be terribly dubious." A good critic and data analyst must do more: he or she must also show *how* the error in the measurement or the analysis affects the inferences made on the basis of that data and analysis. Thus, in this case, two lines of argument are necessary to produce a legitimate statistical criticism. First, it is suggested that states may record deaths from automobile accidents differently. The second step is to suggest a mechanism by which such differences in the recording rate could lead to our present findings. Thus, it is further necessary to suggest not only that states differ in the way they record auto deaths, but also that these differences are related to whether a state has inspections. This seems to be a fair statement, since states with good procedures for analyzing the causes of death in automobile accidents might be those states with activist state governments—indeed, the kind of state governments also likely to have a state inspection program.

3. The response variable is now measured in terms of *per capita* deaths—deaths per 100,000 people living in the state. But the individual driver might be more interested in the risk of death that is assumed for *each mile traveled* along the roads in that state. This reasoning suggests taking a look at the death rate *per hundred million miles* traveled, asking whether inspections reduce the risk of being killed for each mile driven. It turns out that in states with inspections, the death rate is 5.48 deaths per hundred million miles traveled, compared with 5.95 in states without inspections. The inspected states do somewhat better.

An interesting problem arises here in the computation of the mileage death rate. This rate is computed by taking the total number of deaths due to traffic accidents and dividing by the total number of miles traveled in the state. And how is the latter computed? Certainly the number of miles can't be measured directly. Rather, it is known how many gallons of gas are sold in each state, since all states have a gas tax yielding a few cents for each gallon of gas sold. The number of gallons sold are converted into number of miles traveled by assuming that cars get an average of about 12 miles for each gallon of gas. So, the overall computation is

$$\frac{\text{estimate of total}}{\text{miles traveled}} = \frac{\text{revenue from gas tax}}{\text{gas tax rate (cents/gallon)}} \times 12 \text{ miles/gallon.}$$

For example, if the total tax revenue in a state was $1,000,000 and the tax rate was $0.10 per gallon, then 10,000,000 gallons were sold and an estimated 120,000,000 miles were traveled.[11] That is,

$$\frac{\$1,000,000}{\$0.10} \times 12 = 120,000,000.$$

4. Inspections cannot be expected to save all victims of auto accidents, simply because a large share of accidents are not the result of brake failure, bad tires, faulty steering, a missing tail light, or other mechanical defects detected and repaired as a consequence of inspections. A good many crashes are caused by factors that inspections

---

[11] The actual calculation is somewhat more complicated, taking into account evaporation of gasoline, road differences between states, and so forth.

cannot remedy. For example, each year about 1500 people are killed in cars by trains at grade crossings. Probably another 500 die in the course of "hot pursuit" police chases. [12] An unknown (but probably significant) number of people choose the car as their suicide weapon. Finally, inspections will do little to reduce accidents due to drunken driving—and study after study clearly convicts drunken driving as the most important single factor leading to auto accidents. At least half of all fatal crashes involve a driver who had been drinking heavily and had a very high blood alcohol concentration at the time of the crash.

Thus some bias may enter the analysis because states may differ with respect to the proportion of accidents that can be prevented by inspections. Ideally, in the data analyst's heaven, the first step would be to determine the number of accidents *potentially* preventable by inspections and then, by comparing inspected and uninspected states, see whether inspections as currently used actually did prevent the accidents that they should have.

Discussing measurement of the quality of school facilities, Mosteller and Moynihan made the following observations, relevant to our discussion here, about "crude" versus "refined" measures in the study of policy:

> . . . it is the experience of statisticians that when fairly "crude" measurements are refined, the change more often than not turns out to be small. Merely counting the number of laboratories in a school system is, in this sense, a "crude" measurement. It is possible to learn a good deal more about the quality of those laboratories. It could be that on further assessment the judgment to be had from the original crude measurement would be changed. But to repeat, statisticians would not leap too readily to that expectation. . . . Sadly, perhaps, in real life the similarities of basic categories are often far more powerful and important than the nice differences which can come to absorb individuals so disposed, but which really don't make a great difference in the aggregate.
>
> The statistician would wholeheartedly say go ahead and make the better measurements, but he would often give a low probability to the prospect that the finer measures would produce information that would lead to different policy.
>
> The reasons are several. One is that policy decisions are often rather insensitive to the measures—the same policy is often a good one across a great variety of measures. Secondly, the finer measures, as in the case of laboratories, can be thought of as something like

[12]This is a crude estimate; such estimates are obviously difficult to make accurately. See "500 Traffic Deaths Annually Attributed to Police 'Hot Pursuit'," *The New York Times*, June 18, 1968.

weights. For example, perhaps one science laboratory is only half as good as another—well and good, let us count it 1/2. It turns out as an empirical fact that in a great variety of occasions, we get much the same policy decisions in spite of the weights. So there are some technical reasons for thinking that the finer measurement may not change the main thrust of one's policy. None of this is an argument against getting better information if it is needed, or against having reservations. More data cost money, and one has to decide where the good places are to put the next money acquired for investigations. If we think it matters a lot by all means let us measure it better.

Still another point about aggregative statistics is worth emphasizing for large social studies. Although the data may sometimes not be adequate for decisions about individual persons, they may well be adequate for deciding policy for groups. Thus we may not be able to predict which of two ways of teaching spelling will be preferable for a given child, but we may well be able to say that, on the average, a particular method does better. And then the policy is clear, at least until someone learns how to tell which children would do better under the differing methods.[13]

We have observed an association between inspections and lower death rates and have also considered some questions about that relationship. What do these results mean? Are there different explanations of the association between inspections and death rates?

DEVELOPING EXPLANATIONS FOR THE OBSERVED RELATIONSHIP

Many explanatory models begin by working with two variables: a response variable and a single describing variable. Usually, as the analysis develops, additional describing variables come into the model. Let Y denote the response (or dependent) variable and X the describing (or independent) variable. Begin by considering the notion that X causes Y:

$$X \longrightarrow Y.$$

Returning to our example, we sought to find out whether

automobile inspections (X)	$\longrightarrow$	low rate of traffic fatalities. (Y)

[13] From "A Pathbreaking Report," in *On Equality of Educational Opportunity* by Frederick Mosteller and Daniel P. Moynihan, eds. Copyright © 1972 by Random House, Inc. Reprinted by permission of the publisher.

An observed association between two variables can occur for many reasons. There may be a causal relationship between the two variables. The relationship may occur simply by chance. Or X may *covary* with Y because both X and Y are jointly caused by some third factor Z. Thus, the observation that Y increases as X increases is consistent with many explanations.

Once we establish some kind of association between X and Y, the problem is what to make of it. There is supposedly a rather strong association over many years between the salaries of Presbyterian ministers and the price of rum in Havana—yet I doubt that we would want to suggest a causal relationship between the two. The apparent association between the ministers' salaries and the price of rum might arise because both were linked to some extent to the ups and downs of business conditions:

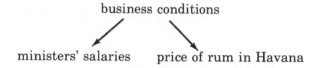

Thus, while salaries and rum prices apparently covary together with great regularity, it is not because ministers are spending their money for rum in Havana, but rather because both salaries and prices are linked to a common, third factor—the business climate. A correlation such as that between ministers' salaries and the price of rum is often called a *spurious correlation;* the relationship is spurious or misleading because the two variables are related only by some third cause.

Is there a possibility that the association between inspections and low death rates is spurious? Do states with both low rates and inspections have some third factor, Z, in common?

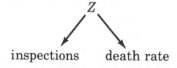

And how do we go about finding likely candidates for this variable Z? Our substantive understanding of the problem may suggest some possible third variables to check for spurious correlation. In other cases, we simply might check through a number of possible variables that seem, for one reason or another, good possibilities. One useful guideline is simply to ask: What other factors are related to either X or Y? In other words, are there any variables closely linked to

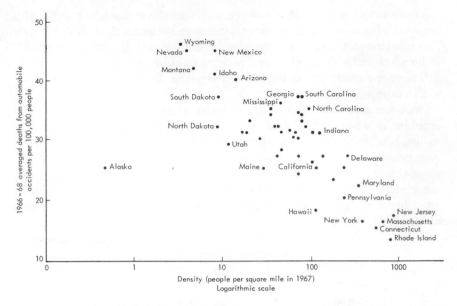

FIGURE 1-5   Death rate and density

death rate—and if so, are they also linked to the presence or absence of inspections?

In looking for other such variables, we turn up several candidates: the density of the state, its weather conditions, and the percentage of young drivers. The density (number of people per square mile) is strongly related to the death rate: as the density of a state increases, the death rate decreases. In other words, thickly populated states such as Connecticut and New Jersey have low death rates from automobile accidents; thinly populated states such as Nevada and Wyoming have high rates. Figure 1-5 shows the relations between density and death rate for the fifty states.[14] Such a pattern indicates a negative relationship, since the variables vary inversely; that is, as X gets bigger and bigger, Y tends to get smaller and smaller. States of *high* density, then, have *low* death rates; and states of *low* density have *high* rates. The scatterplot reveals a rather strong relationship between density and death rate, since the states progress in a relatively orderly fashion across the scatterplot.

Thinly populated states have higher fatality rates compared to thickly populated states because drivers go for longer distances at

[14] Density is plotted on a logarithmic scale in Figure 1–5 for reasons explained in Chapter 3. Alaska has been dropped from further analysis because of its atypical nature differing apparently from the other 49 states.

higher speeds in the less dense states. Accidents in states like Nevada and Arizona are probably typically more severe since they occur at a higher speed. It is not, however, just a matter of the number of miles driven, because there is also a fairly strong negative relationship between density and the *deaths per 100 million miles driven* in the state. Victims of accidents in the more thinly populated states, in addition to being involved in more severe accidents, are also less likely to be discovered and treated immediately, since both Good Samaritans and hospitals are more scattered in thinly populated states compared to the denser states.

Is the correlation between inspections of automobiles and low traffic death rates spurious? Given the strong relationship between density and the death rate, might there also be a relationship between density and the presence or absence of safety inspections? Are the high-density states (with their low death rates) more likely to have inspections? It looks that way; eight of the nine most thickly populated states have inspections, as compared with only one of the eight least dense states. This preliminary look suggests that the model

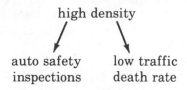

high density

auto safety   low traffic
inspections   death rate

has some merit.

The density of a state's population certainly doesn't directly cause auto safety inspections. But a plausible argument explains the relationship between the two: the denser states tend to be the urbanized, industrialized, northeastern, politically competitive states with activist state governments—governments that would be more likely to inaugurate an inspection program. Looking at the data will help decide whether the relationship between inspections and reduced death rates is a spurious one resulting from the common element of density. To find out whether inspections have an effect, discounting the influence of density on the death rate, we will want to compare states at a similar level of density to see whether inspected states have lower death rate than uninspected states. To put it another way, it is necessary to hold density constant in order to observe the uncluttered (by density) effects of inspections on accident deaths.

Two different methods, *matching* and *adjustment,* help take into account the effects of density. Let us try it both ways here.

Matching simply involves taking states of roughly the same density and seeing whether inspected states have lower rates than uninspected states within the density groupings. States are matched, then, with respect to density; often this procedure is called "controlling for" density. Table 1-1, comparing the average death rate for inspected and uninspected states for thinly, moderately, and thickly populated states, shows:

1. The averaged death rates are lowest in the thickly populated states and highest in the thinly populated states, regardless of whether they have inspections or not (in other words, the averaged rates decrease as we read across either the inspected-states row or the uninspected-states row).
2. At each level of density (thin, medium, and thick) the average death rate for the inspected states is lower than for uninspected states.

The average death rate for each of the six cells is computed by adding up the rates for the states in given cell and dividing by the number of states in the cell. This average or mean rate is very sensitive to extreme values; for example, for the thinly populated states with inspections, the three states have the rates 28.8, 30.9, and 45.0. New Mexico, at 45.0, forces the average up to almost 35, even though two of the three states are actually close to 30.

The division and assignment of states into three categories is perfectly arbitrary. Many other divisions are probably just as good. Table 1-2 shows a slightly different set of categories; it differs somewhat from Table 1-1 because the shuffling of a few states from one category to another affects the averages to some extent. Table 1-2, like Table 1-1, however, shows that some relationship remains between inspections and a reduced death rate even when the effects of density are controlled.

The matching procedure often helps inform the reader what is going on in the data: Tables 1-1 and 1-2 clearly display the effect of inspections at the three density levels and also the effect of density at each inspection level. Matching has some defects, chiefly that it is difficult to do a very good job of matching in complex situations without a large number of cases. In Table 1-1 we have not really matched the states in a very satisfactory way by throwing them into three bins labeled "thin," "moderate," and "thick." A good deal of variation density remains within each of the three levels of density. For instance, both Wyoming (density = 3.2 people per square mile) and Oregon (density = 20.8) are described as "thinly populated," although they differ widely in density. Thus by putting the states into only three categories we lose some information about one of the key variables (density). Before

TABLE 1-1

Inspections, Density, and Average Death Rates

	Density					
	Thin		Medium		Thick	
	Average	N	Average	N	Average	N
States without inspections	38.5	9	31.5	16	23.6	6
States with inspections	34.9	3	28.4	9	18.3	6

Definitions:

Thin   = density less than or equal to 25 people per square mile.
Medium = more than 25 and less than 125 people per square mile.
Thick   = 125 or more people per square mile.
Average = mean death rate for states in that category (computed by adding up the death rates for all the states in that category and dividing by the number of states in that category).
N   = number of states in that category.
Total   = 49 states (all states except Alaska).

ORIGINAL DATA (STATES AND THEIR DEATH RATES)

Density

	Thin		Medium		Thick	
States without inspections	Arizona	38.8	Alabama	31.2	Connecticut	14.7
	Idaho	40.2	Arkansas	34.2	Illinois	23.0
	Montana	42.2	California	25.4	Indiana	31.1
	Nebraska	30.5	Florida	31.4	Maryland	22.0
	Nevada	45.4	Georgia	36.9	Michigan	26.5
	North Dakota	31.7	Iowa	31.3	Ohio	24.5
	Oregon	33.3	Kansas	30.0		
	South Dakota	37.0	Kentucky	33.0		
	Wyoming	48.0	Minnesota	27.7		
			Missouri	30.5		
			North Carolina	35.1		
			Oklahoma	35.0		
			South Carolina	36.6		
			Tennessee	31.5		
			Washington	28.1		
			Wisconsin	27.4		
States with inspections	Colorado	30.9	Louisiana	34.1	Delaware	27.0
	New Mexico	45.0	Maine	24.7	Massachusetts	16.4
	Utah	28.8	Mississippi	36.0	New Jersey	17.3
			New Hampshire	23.8	New York	16.1
			Texas	31.5	Pennsylvania	19.8
			Vermont	32.0	Rhode Island	13.0
			West Virginia	30.1		
			Virginia	26.0		
			Hawaii	17.8		

TABLE 1-2

Inspections, Density (Different Division), and Average Death Rates

	Thin		Medium		Thick	
	Average	N	Average	N	Average	N
States without inspections	37.6	11	32.1	11	26.0	9
States with inspections	32.4	4	31.2	6	19.2	8

Identical to Table 1-1 except:

Thin   = density less or equal to than 37 people per square mile.
Medium = more than 37 and less than 100 people per square mile.
Thick   = 100 or more people per square mile.

classifying both Wyoming and Oregon as thinly populated, we knew that they differed by such-and-such amount in their densities. But now, in Table 1-1, this information is not used in the analysis, and the two states are treated as if they were alike. The situation is just as troubling for the states in the thickly populated category. Here, the states range from a density of 138.3 people per square mile in Indiana up to New Jersey with 929.8.

One limitation of matching, then, is that quite often the match is not very accurate. A second limitation is that if we want to control for more than one variable using matching procedures, the tables begin to have combinations of categories without any cases at all in them, and they become somewhat more difficult for the reader to understand. For example, if states were matched with respect to density (three categories in this case) and, in addition, their weather (say five categories), the fifty states would be scattered over fifteen different combinations of density and weather conditions (and some combinations might not even exist empirically—for example, a warm, dry state that was also densely populated). When the inspection classification was added, the fifty states would then be classified into thirty categories. The scattering of cases over many different cells (or combinations of different levels of variables) of the table can be avoided by collapsing categories (using, say, two levels of density instead of three)—but then, of course, states become less and less well matched, and the effects of density are less well controlled because of the wide variations in density in supposedly "matched" groups.

Adjustment, the other procedure for controlling the effects of a third variable, sometimes partially overcomes these difficulties. By standardizing the death rate of each state for the density of that

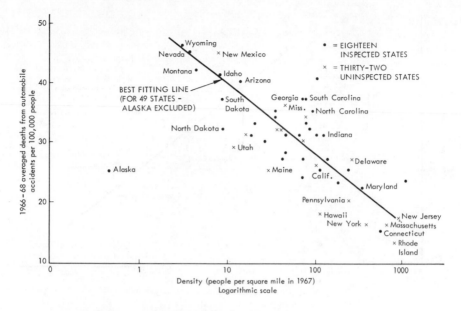

FIGURE 1-6   Fitted line: death rate and density

state, the adjustment procedure takes out the effect of density on the death rate, producing what might be called a "density-standardized death rate." We can employ the procedure informally merely by looking at the scatterplot (Figure 1-6), which shows the plot of the death rate against density for the inspected and uninspected states. The line fitted to the points here is the line that best fits the relationship between density and deaths.

The line makes what is essentially an average prediction: given that a state has a certain density, the line predicts that state's death rate. Some states lie below the prediction line, indicating that they have a lower death rate than predicted by their density. States that lie above the line have a higher death rate than predicted. If inspected states have a lower death rate—for their density level—than uninspected states, then they should tend to lie below the line and below the point representing the uninspected states in the same region of density on the scatterplot. In other words, the little circles (representing the inspected states) should, at a given density level, tend to lie below the x's (representing the uninspected states) if inspections have an effect after controlling for density. Although no vivid effect appears in Figure 1-6, it is possible to see a slight tendency indicating lower rates in inspected states.

Let us now formalize the adjustment procedure and take out the

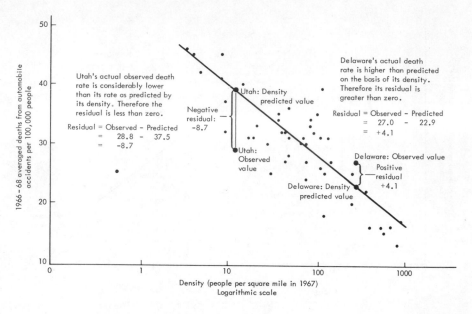

FIGURE 1-7   Residuals from fitted line

effects of density mathematically. The line fitted to the points represents the predicted death rate for a given density. Thus for each
state there is a predicted death rate—a prediction based on its density.
Also, we know the *actual* death rate in each state. The difference
between the actual, observed death rate for a state and the predicted
death rate represents that part of the death rate that is unaccounted
for by the state's density. The difference between the observed and
the predicted death rate is called the *residual:*

| residual for a given state | = | actual observed death rate for that state | − | predicted (by density) death rate for that state |

Thus the residuals for all the states are computed simply by subtracting
the density-predicted death rate from the actual rate.[15] Each residual
can be viewed as a death rate adjusted for density; it is that part
of the death rate that is unexplained by density. Figure 1-7 shows
the logic. Generating a predicted death on the basis of density and
then examining the residual death rate is, in effect, a statistical

[15] The computational method is described in Chapter 3.

way of matching or equating all states with respect to density. The examination of residuals is a powerful tool for the analysis of data, since the residual represents that part of the variation in the response variable that remains unexplained after looking at a set of describing variables. The residuals measure what remains to be explained in the response variable. New explanations can be developed by seeing how the residuals are related to other describing variables. Examples and further details are found in Chapters 3 and 4.

Figure 1-8 shows the residuals (or the density-adjusted death rates) for the inspected and the uninspected states. Generally, those states with a lower death rate than expected are those states that have inspections—with Mississippi, Louisiana, and New Mexico being very prominent exceptions. On the average, states with inspections have a rate 1.63 deaths per 100,000 people *lower* than expected and states without inspections have a rate of 0.90 deaths per 100,000 population *higher* than expected—yielding a difference of 2.5 deaths per 100,000 between inspected and uninspected states after adjustment of the rates for density. While the difference is neither large nor sure, it does favor inspections. The difference might suggest that if inspections were implemented by all states, perhaps an additional 2500 lives would be saved each year. This is far from certain. Greater certainty might be obtained by taking other variables into account. But to increase substantially the credibility of the view that inspections make a difference would require a well-designed experiment. The nonexperimental data examined here can only give small hints about what is going on.

Compulsory inspections of automobiles, by getting some mechanical defects straightened out, might produce a modest reduction in the death rate from car crashes. If intervention at the level of the car owner has effects of the size observed in this study, then what additional measures, beyond inspections, might cut the death and injury rate from automobile accidents? As mentioned earlier, efforts to reduce drunken driving may be helpful. But safety efforts at the level of the individual driver are limited; as Moynihan wrote:

> There is not much evidence that the number of accidents can be substantially reduced simply by altering the behavior of drivers while maintaining a near universal driving population. It may be this can be done, but it has not been done. This leads to the basic strategy of crash injury protection: it is assumed that a great many automobile accidents will continue to occur. That being the case, the most efficient way to minimize the overall cost of accidents is to design the interior of the vehicles so that the *injuries* that follow the *accidents* are relatively mild. An attraction of this approach is that it could be

28

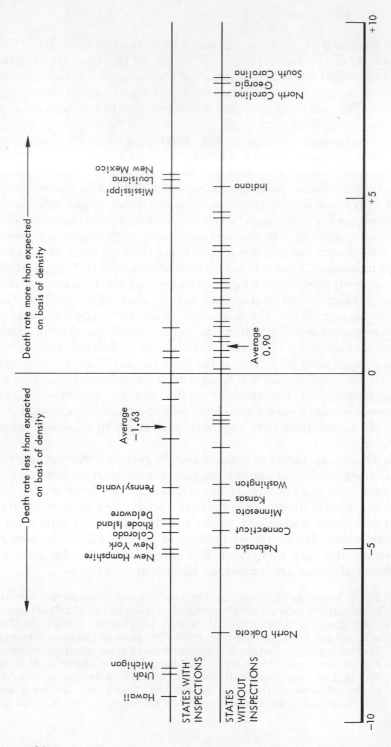

FIGURE 1-8 Residuals—the density-adjusted death rate—for inspected and uninspected states

put into effect by changing the behavior of a tiny population—the forty or fifty executives who run the automobile industry.[16]

COSTS AND UNQUANTIFIABLE ASPECTS

To conclude let us briefly consider some of the costs of inspections and look at some aspects of the problem that are not quantifiable.

Inspections, as noted earlier, have significant costs. Almost all of these costs, direct and indirect, fall on the individual car owner. Inspections, therefore, produce few pressures on or incentives for automobile manufacturers to build safer cars free of mechanical defects. Under an inspection system, if the headlights of a car are misaligned in the factory or if a tail light burns out, the car owner pays the cost of fixing the defect when it is discovered in the inspection. Not only is there no cost to the manufacturer for having produced a car with a defect, but indeed there is a further profit to be made on the replacement part correcting the defect. Thus inspections are a limited strategy for coping with car crashes because of their modest effects, their significant costs, and their failure—if it may be called that—to snowball into further safety efforts.

Earlier, some crude estimates of the economic costs of inspections were given—the figure running to perhaps $500 million in those states with inspections. There are also political and social costs of programs (such as inspections) which require coercion by the threat of arrest and fine of large number of citizens (in this case, 80 million car owners). While the total experiences of most citizens with their government occur in similarly coercive and bureaucratic contexts— such as the income tax, the draft, traffic tickets, and auto licensing— what are, in fact, the long-run costs of bureaucratic and arbitrary impingements upon citizens by the government? Do some citizens consequently become alienated and cynical about its performance? Does the modest coercion involved in inspection programs lead to the eventual acceptance of increasingly more severe coercion?

Since it is difficult to measure certain kinds of political and social costs, as well as benefits, of a program, such unmeasurable factors sometimes receive less emphasis than they should. (On the other hand, bizarre estimates of such costs may go unchallenged for the lack of data to prove them wrong.) For example, in the judicial process, it is easy to measure police performance in terms of the numbers of arrests made; but it is more difficult to assess performance with respect to equal or fair treatment. Or, to take another example, the

[16]Moynihan, *op. cit.*, p. 12.

apparently huge costs of smoking cigarettes—the years of life lost to early death, the excess illness among smokers, the fires started by smoking—have been measured carefully and extensively in the last twenty years. In contrast, the gratification received from smoking by the smoker cannot be ascertained; and presumably such information has at least modest relevance to decisions about public policy toward smoking.

Our inability to measure important factors does not mean either that we should sweep those factors under the rug or that we should give them all the weight in a decision. Some important factors in some problems can be assessed quantitatively. And even though thoughtful and imaginative efforts have sometimes turned the "unmeasurable" into a useful number, some important factors are simply not measurable. As always, every bit of the investigator's ingenuity and good judgment must be brought into play. And, whatever unknowns may remain, the analysis of quantitative data nonetheless can help us learn something about the world—even if it is not the whole story.

CHAPTER 2

Predictions and Projections:
Some Issues of
Research Design

"There will be no nuclear war within the next fifty years."

"In the period 1965–70, Mao Tse-tung and De Gaulle will die."

"Major fighting in Viet-Nam will peter out about 1967; and most objective observers will regard it as a substantial American victory."

"In the United States Lyndon Johnson will have been re-elected in 1968."

—Ithiel de Sola Pool[1]

Introduction

Projections of the future can be useful or embarrassing, depending on their accuracy. The assumption that a wide range of factors remain constant or continue to change at current rates can quickly crumble.[2] And yet how imbedded in our thought is the idea that the future is a straightforward projection of the past: we may doubt the optimism of Professor Pool's first prediction if only because of the failure of the other predictions on the list. At least, unlike some predictions, these have the modest virtue of being explicit, and it is easy to tell whether they went wrong.[3]

---

[1] "The International System in the Next Half Century," in Daniel Bell, ed., *Toward the Year 2000: Work in Progress* (Boston: Beacon Press, 1967), pp. 319–20.

[2] A very useful discussion of the assumptions behind many projections is Otis Dudley Duncan, "Social Forecasting—The State of the Art," *The Public Interest*, no. 17 (Fall 1969), 88–118.

[3] On previous prophecies, see Arthur M. Schlesinger, "Casting the National Horoscope," *Proceedings of the American Antiquarian Society*, 55 (1945), 53–93.

Almost all efforts at data analysis seek, at some point, to generalize the results and extend the reach of the conclusions beyond a particular set of data. The inferential leap may be from past experiences to future ones, from a sample of a population to the whole population, or from a narrow range of a variable to a wider range. The real difficulty is in deciding when the extrapolation beyond the range

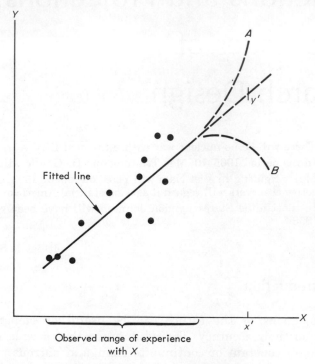

FIGURE 2-1   Problem of simple extrapolation

Q: Should the fitted line be extended to predict the value y' for the new observation x' (which is outside the range of previous experience with the x-variable)? Or, is A or B a better model?

A: "*A priori* nonstatistical considerations . . ."

of the variables is warranted and when it is merely naive. As usual, it is largely a matter of substantive judgment—or, as it is sometimes more delicately put, a matter of "a priori nonstatistical considerations" (Figure 2-1).

If the observed variation in a variable is small relative to its total possible variation, then the extension of the inference based on a narrow range of observations is less warranted than extrapolation based on a wider range of observed variations. Equally obvious is the observation that the risk of error is less if the extrapolated value is "close" to the previous pattern of experience rather than greatly different, other things being equal. In some cases it may be useful to conduct trial runs at extrapolation by using a fraction of the available data to produce a fitted curve, using the remaining data to test the accuracy of the extrapolated results. Obviously if the conditions governing a relationship change in relevant respects, the effort at extension of results is in danger of making errors.

Simple extrapolation involves the extension of results outside the range of experience of a single describing variable. A more subtle situation arises in the multivariate case involving extrapolation beyond the range of the *combination* of experience jointly observed in two or more describing variables. Karl A. Fox has described this situation as "hidden extrapolation."[4]

Figure 2-2 shows the pattern of correlation between two describing variables. Assume these two describing variables, X_1 and X_2, are used in combination to predict a response variable, Y. The situation appears to be relatively satisfactory because there is a wide range of experience with both X_1 and X_2. But note how little experience there is concerning certain *combinations* of X_1 and X_2—since all the points representing joint occurrences of X_1 and X_2 are contained in the narrow band surrounding the line. There is no experience with combinations such as low X_1-high X_2 (in the upper left of the rectangle) or high X_1-low X_2 (lower left) and how such unobserved combinations of X_1 and X_2 might affect the response variable. The response variable may behave very differently for such combinations of X_1 and X_2. Thus a prediction equation, predicting Y from X_1 and X_2, may be quite misleading if applied to situations in which X_1 and X_2 occur in combinations different from those observed here.

Thus the extension of the inference over all combinations of X_1 and X_2 may founder on the possibility of an interaction effect between X_1 and X_2 in their influence on Y in the region of the combinations with which there is no experience. The problem arises because of limited experience with the *joint* relationship of X_1 and X_2, even though there may be extensive experience with the entire range of each variable taken singly. Thus the name, "hidden extrapolation."

The problem arises in any predictive study involving correlated describing variables. Figure 2-3 shows the narrowed range of joint experience in the case of three correlated describing variables.

We diagnose the problem by considering the scatterplots of the

[4]This discussion is based on Karl A. Fox, *Intermediate Economic Statistics* (New York: Wiley, 1968), pp. 265–66.

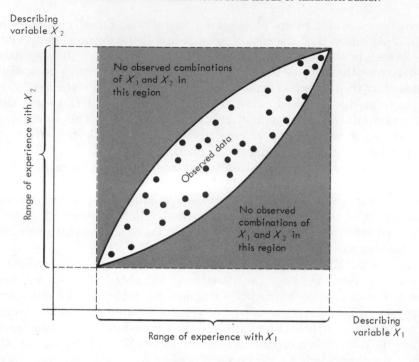

FIGURE 2-2   Correlation between two describing variables

relationships between the describing variables and by looking over the original joint observations. Cures for the difficulty include the collection of additional data, particularly of "deviant cases" in areas outside the previously experienced combinations of describing variables.

Let us now turn to several examples illustrating and evaluating methods of prediction. These case studies show different statistical tools in action. Note, however, that the central consideration in most cases is the research design, rather than the mechanics of using the statistical tool. Mosteller and Bush make this point quite sharply:

> We first wish to emphasize that formal statistics provides the investigator with tools useful in conducting thoughtful research; these tools are not a substitute for either thinking or working. A major goal for the statistical training of students should be statistical thinking rather than statistical formulas, by which we mean specifically: thinking about (1) the conception and design of the study and what it is that is to be measured and why, (2) the definitions of the terms being used, and how modifications in definition might change both the outcome and the interpretation of a study, (3) sources of variation in every part of the study, including such things as

individual differences, group and race differences, environmental differences, instrumental or measuring errors, and intrinsic variation fundamental to the process under investigation. In no circumstances do we think that sophisticated analytical devices should replace clean design and careful execution, unless very unusual economic considerations arise. However, it may be worth remarking that crude data collected as best the investigator could may require the most advanced statistical tools. Here a quotation from Wallis may be appropriate:

> In general, if a statistical investigation . . . is well planned and the data properly collected the interpretation will pretty well take care of itself. So-called "high-powered," "refined," or "elaborate" statistical techniques are generally called for when the data are crude and inadequate— exactly the opposite, if I may be permitted an obiter dictum, of what crude and inadequate statisticians usually think."[5]

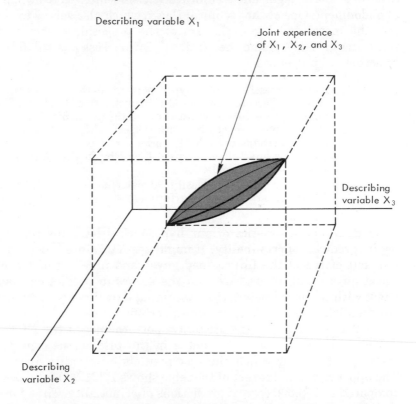

FIGURE 2-3   Range of joint experience—three describing variables

[5] Frederick Mosteller and Robert R. Bush, "Selected Quantitative Techniques," in Gardner Lindzey, ed., Handbook of Social Psychology: Vol. I, Theory and Method (Cambridge, Mass.: Addison-Wesley, 1954), p. 331. The passage by Wallis is found in W. Allen Wallis, "Statistics of the Kinsey Report," Journal of the American Statistical Association, 44 (1949), p. 471.

Problem in Prediction: The National Crime Test and a Cancer Test

Assessing the quality of a prediction or extrapolation can sometimes be a tricky matter. Consider the following example, which reveals the interplay between the properties of the predictive device and the tested population.

A proposal was once made that every 6-, 7-, and 8-year-old child (a total of 13 million in all) be given psychological tests to identify potential "criminality" in order that the supposed lawbreakers of the future be given some sort of treatment. The proposal encountered a storm of moral, legal, and technical criticism which led to its apparent abandonment. One of the technical flaws, which also serves to emphasize the moral and legal criticism of the proposal, is shown in the following model. Assume the National Crime Test has the following hypothetical properties:

1. It will successfully identify 40 percent of those arrested in the future. (Unfortunately, a child's "identification" by the NCT might help insure his future arrest through the mechanism of a self-fulfilling prophecy, operating with respect to the child or the police or both. Perhaps even NCT scores would be used to convince a jury of the guilt of the accused—thereby further increasing the "accuracy" of the prediction.)
2. It will also correctly classify 90 percent of those children who will not be arrested in the future.

Do these characteristics of our hypothetical NCT indicate it is a useful predictor of criminality? It might seem so, since it does identify four out of ten of the future "bad guys" and nine out of ten of the "good guys." But let us look into the errors in prediction made by a test with these characteristics. Assuming that three percent of these children will, later in life, commit a serious crime, we can construct Table 2-1, which shows the predictive performance of the NCT.

The table shows the errors made in the test; let us consider the "false positives" in which the test predicts criminality incorrectly. The upper righthand corner of the table shows 1,261,000 false positives compared to 156,000 correct predictions of criminality. Thus for every correct prediction of future difficulties, there are eight incorrect ones! In this light, such a test would be unacceptable to most people—even though its predictive characteristics, as originally expressed, seemed impressive. Furthermore, the assumptions we made about the predictive powers of such tests were, if anything, much too generous, given the poor performance of psychological tests of "criminality."

TABLE 2-1
Hypothetical (Fortunately) National Crime Test

		Reality	
		Criminal	Noncriminal
Test predicts	Criminal	156,000	1,261,000
	Noncriminal	234,000	11,349,000
		390,000	12,610,000
		Total = 13,000,000	

COMPUTATIONS:
3 percent of 13,000,000 children will commit a serious crime:
    (.03)(13,000,000) = 390,000 children. NCT accurately predicts 40 percent:
    (.40)(390,000) = 156,000
97 percent of 13,000,000 are not future criminals:
    (.97)(13,000,000) = 12,610,000. NCT accurately predicts 90 percent:
    (.90)(12,610,000) = 11,349,000.

Consider another example of the same problem. A hypothetical test for cancer has the following characteristics:

1. Pr(test positive | cancer) = .95. This conditional probability indicates that the test reads "positive" 95 percent of the time given that the person tested in fact has cancer.
2. Pr(test negative | no cancer) = .96.

In other words, the test correctly identifies, on the average, 95 out of 100 of those who do have cancer and also 96 out of 100 of those who do not have cancer. These characteristics give the following table of probabilities:

		Reality	
		Cancer	No cancer
Test predicts	Positive	.95	.04
	Negative	.05	.96
		1.00	1.00

Now assume that one percent of those tested actually do have cancer; that is, Pr(cancer) = .01. (This is an unconditional probability, since it depends upon no given prior condition.) Note that since only one percent of those tested have cancer, the flow of those tested is mainly down the righthand column of the table of probabilities.

What proportion of false positives (and false negatives) will be

TABLE 2-2
Computation of Probabilities

We have the following data:
Pr(cancer) = .01
Therefore Pr(not cancer) = 1.00 − .01 = .99.
Similarly,
Pr(test positive | cancer) = .95, and therefore
Pr(test negative | cancer) = .05.
Also,
Pr(test negative | no cancer) = .96, and therefore
Pr(test positive | no cancer) = .04.

The problem is to compute Pr(cancer | test positive), which equals, by Bayes' theorem:

$$\frac{\text{Pr(test positive | cancer) Pr(cancer)}}{\text{Pr(test positive | cancer) Pr(cancer) + Pr(test positive | not cancer) Pr(not cancer)}}$$
$$= \frac{(.95)(.01)}{(.95)(.01) + (.04)(96)} = .19.$$

---

produced by the test? One way to answer with respect to false positives is to compute Pr(cancer | test positive)—the probability that a person has cancer, given that the test reads positive. This can be done, using the appropriate equations for conditional probabilities, shown in Table 2-2. Another way to handle the problem is to consider what happens when, say, 10,000 people are screened for cancer using the hypothetical test. Computations analogous to those in Table 2-1 yield the following expected results:

		Reality	
		Cancer	*No cancer*
Test predicts	*Positive*	95	396
	Negative	5	9,504

and therefore

$$\text{Pr(cancer | positive)} = \frac{95}{95 + 396} = .19.$$

Thus about 19 percent of those indicated positive will actually have cancer; 81 percent of the positives will be false. The decision whether this is a good test depends upon the cost of such false positives and their consequent detection as well as the benefits that derive from the detection of the disease. Perhaps such a test would be most useful as a screening device to indicate patients needing further tests.

Similar arguments apply to the use of lie detectors, the prediction of juvenile delinquency on the basis of family background, and the use of "preventive detention."[6] The reason the original qualities of the prediction seem to collapse when the test is applied to data is that, in these two cases, the quality to be detected is rather rare. Therefore, even though the hypothetical cancer test correctly predicts cancer 95 percent of the time and noncancer 96 percent of the time, so many people (99 percent in our example) flow through the right (noncancer) side of the table of probabilities that even the low error *rate* (4 percent) produces a large *number* of errors *relative* to the number of correct predictions of cancer. If, on the other hand, *half* the tested population had cancer, then the expected table (for 10,000 people) would be:

		Reality	
		Cancer	*No Cancer*
	Positive	4750	200
Test predicts			
	Negative	250	4800

This is pretty sensational predicting!

The *properties of the test are the same* in both cases, but the populations tested differ with respect to the distribution of the characteristic to be detected. Thus a test which does a good job of prediction on one population may not perform so well on a second trial if distribution of the characteristic sought differs markedly in the second population. Thus it will be worthwhile to try out—if only by working through the arithmetic as we have done here—the test on a population for which the distribution of the characteristic to be predicted is the same as the population for which the ultimate prediction is to be made. Note that the two numbers Pr(positive | cancer) and Pr(negative | not cancer) were not enough to describe adequately the performance of the prediction. Instead, a third piece of information, in this case Pr(cancer), was necessary to permit an adequate assessment of the performance of the test for that population.

[6]See Jerome H. Skolnick, "Scientific Theory and Scientific Evidence: An Analysis of Lie-Detection," *Yale Law Journal*, 70 (April 1961), 694–728; and Travis Hirschi and Hanan C. Selvin, *Delinquency Research* (New York: Free Press, 1967), chap. 14.

Finally, some very high rates of successful "prediction" should not fool us. After all, we can achieve 99 percent "accuracy" simply by predicting that no person has cancer. Since 99 percent of the people in our example don't have cancer, the rule is 99 percent "accurate" in a sense, although next to worthless medically.

Election-Night Forecasting

Each election night, when the polls have closed and the votes are being counted, the three television networks forecast the electoral outcome on the basis of early, partial returns—often needing only a few percent of the vote to predict accurately the final outcome. The networks invest millions of dollars in their electoral coverage, which allows their viewers to learn the results of the election several hours earlier than they might otherwise. Although this is perhaps a small yield for the investment, the scramble for early returns needed for the projection of the winner might, in some places in some elections, discourage corrupt election officials from greatly altering the real count of the vote—since the pressure of getting the vote count in may reduce the time needed to fix the returns.

For example, pressures for a timely count may curb such abuses as those in Illinois in the 1968 tabulation:

> For days before the election, the Chicago papers were full of tales of heavy crops of bums and derelicts being registered in West Side flophouses to provide the names for a fine Democratic turnout. And suspicion became certainty in the press rooms . . . when it was learned that "computer breakdowns" and "disputed vote counts" were holding the Illinois decision back. Veteran reporters could be heard explaining . . . how the game was played in Illinois: how both the iron Mayor and his Republican enemies downstate would "hold back" hundreds of precincts in an effort to finesse each other to give a hint of the size of the total they had to beat; how they would release a few precincts as bait to lure the other man into giving away some of his. . . .[7]

This suggests that the count of the vote is a rather unusual statistic. For most social and economic indicators, there is a tradeoff between timeliness and accuracy: the quicker we get the information, the greater the error. Sometimes the making of economic policy has been based on very short-run economic statistics—with a resulting reliance

---

[7] Lewis Chester, Godfrey Hodgson, and Bruce Page, *An American Melodrama: The Presidential Campaign of 1968* (New York: Viking, 1969), pp. 760–61.

on less accurate statistics—and more accurate figures might well have produced a different policy. In contrast to the usual case, however, a slow count of the vote often indicates vote fraud, or at least the opportunity for vote fraud.[8]

Although they may, in passing, reduce vote fraud, the central concern of the networks is to forecast the winner of the election (and, secondarily, the winner's share of the vote) on the basis of scattered and very incomplete returns. Two methods, both interpreting early returns with reference to a historical baseline drawn from previous elections, have been favored: (1) comparison of tonight's returns with the returns from previous elections at the same stage of the count and (2) comparison of tonight's returns from various counties with the returns from previous elections from those same counties.

The first method begins by constructing, on the basis of a previous election, a curve showing the relationship between the proportion of the vote reported and the proportion of the reported vote for the Democratic (or Republican) candidate. Figure 2-4 shows one such pattern, indicating that in this case a Democratic candidate who has more than about 40 percent of the vote when less than about 70 percent of the vote has reported can expect to win rather easily when all the returns are in. Such a pattern might result from the early reporting of certain Republican areas and a slower count in heavily Democratic areas. Thus the curve—called a "mu curve"—helps adjust for the bias favoring one party or the other in the sequence of early returns. Figure 2-5 indicates how this might be done. Tonight's returns are compared with the historical pattern of reporting, an appropriate adjustment for reporting bias is made, and the final projection is put on the air. In practice, the method is fancied up a bit—but still its basic defect persists: it relies on the assumption that the order in which the vote is reported remains the same from election to election. This assumption has led to several predictive disasters, and now mu curves only supplement other, more solidly based techniques.

One such predictive botch occurred during an election when a heavily Republican state first introduced voting machines. As a result, that state's flood of Republican ballots came in hours earlier than usual; the mu curve, believing that these were the same votes it saw in each election every four years, quickly projected a Republican landslide for president. Hours and hours later, John Kennedy won one of the closest presidential contests in history.

[8]The problem of inaccurate counts of the vote is not unimportant; political observers guess that two or three million votes are stolen, miscounted, or changed in a U.S. presidential election. Nobody has a good guess about the partisan advantage, if any, resulting from stolen votes. The advantage differs by state.

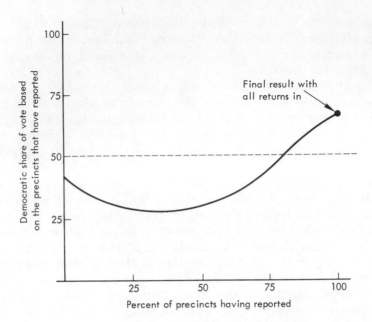

FIGURE 2-4   Historical pattern of the vote as more and more precincts
report their returns on election night

Some practitioners patch up their mu curves by taking into account
expected changes in the order of reporting:

> In deriving mu curves which are empirical in nature—they have
> to be—one must take into very careful consideration whether or
> not there have been any changes in voting patterns resulting from
> voting machines, or changes in poll closing times. Where there are
> such changes—and in every election we find that there are some—the
> mu curves have to be suitably adjusted in order to render them
> suitable.[9]

This sort of repair requires knowledge *in advance* of those changes
in election procedures that might affect the sequence of the vote
report—and must then guess how much earlier or later the affected
returns will show up in the reporting sequence. The method also
rests on the fragile hope that the patched-up curve traced out by
tonight's returns will flow parallel to the historical curve—an assumption that will not hold up if there is a differential shift in particular

[9] Jack Moshman, "Mathematical and Computational Considerations of the
Election Night Projection Program," paper presented at the Spring Joint Computer
Conference in Atlantic City, N.J., on May 2, 1968, p. 3.

areas to a particular candidate. For example, if areas that normally report late and also normally vote somewhat Democratic suddenly shift very strongly toward the Democratic candidate because of that candidate's special appeal in those areas, then the paths traced out by the historical curve and tonight's curve would not be parallel, and the projection might be wrong. Finally, the method does not easily accommodate new political factors, such as a third-party candidate.

Because of these limitations and the availability of more powerful, more inferentially secure methods, mu curves are not now widely used in electoral projections, although they do retain some utility for informal use in interpreting election returns. That utility comes from the limited insight upon which mu curves are based: that different areas, with different voting patterns, report their returns at different times on election evening. Of course we knew that anyway.

The second—and preferred—forecasting method compares tonight's returns from those counties (or wards, precincts, or the like) that have reported early with the returns from previous elections in those same counties. The adjustment of current returns by previous per-

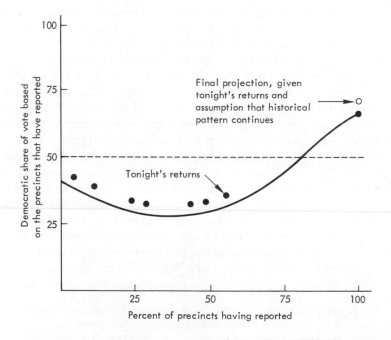

FIGURE 2-5 Comparing tonight's returns with the historical pattern to make a projection

formance at a disaggregated level (that is, at the county level) requires more detailed data and analysis than the mu-curve method—but it yields far more inferentially secure results. That is, there is a good chance that we know more after having done the analysis than we did before.

Comparing tonight's returns from a county with its previous voting patterns takes into account that the counties reporting first are not a representative sample. Counties with early complete returns may tend, in some states, to be Republican counties; in others, Democratic counties. At any rate, why hope they are typical or representative? Comparing current returns with old returns will adjust or control for a county's normal political leanings. For example, the raw returns from Massachusetts are not very helpful in projecting the national winner in a presidential race; but such returns are helpful if we know that Massachusetts normally runs heavily Democratic. So, if the Democratic candidate barely leads in Massachusetts, then that candidate is surely in real trouble nationwide.

Note the assumption here that the shift or the swing toward one party is roughly the same over the whole state or the whole nation. This assumption will not however lead to disaster—because it can be checked on election night with the data in hand simply by comparing the shifts across the counties that have reported. If the shifts are not consistent across counties, then either the historical base values from previous elections for the counties are ill-chosen and inappropriate for judging the pattern of tonight's election, or else the candidates had a special appeal to certain groups clustered by region and the shifts are not the same for different parts of the country. In contrast, violations of assumptions behind the mu-curve method are not easily discovered—at least in the short-run on election night.

Thus the second projection method is somewhat more powerful and safer than the use of mu curves because its assumptions are more modest and because some of its important assumptions can be verified during the course of the analysis. The second method does, however, require much more data and computing power; the grand assumptions of the mu curves are replaced by the collection and analysis of data.

In practice, the final projection of the election consists of a combination of several separate projections. This mixture forming the final, aggregate projection melds several component projections together:

1. the projection from the method of county-adjusted returns: $\%D_c$ = percent Democratic projected from counties;
2. the projection resulting from the so-called "key precincts," which are chosen either randomly or because of their special political

interest: $\%D_k$ = percent Democratic projected from key precincts;
3. the projection of the race before any returns are in at all, called a "prior"—a projection based on pre-election polls or political judgment: $\%D_p$ = prior projection of percent Democratic.

How much of each projection is mixed into the overall combined or "meld" projection? The prior, of course, receives full weight when no returns are in; as the returns pile up, the prior should carry less and less weight in the meld projection. Figure 2-6 shows one such weighting plan, with the weight, $w(r)$, a function of the number of precincts reporting. How should the other factors, $\%D_c$ and $\%D_k$, be weighted in the grand meld projection? Statisticians have a standard answer: form a weighted average using the reciprocal of the variances for weights.

Reciprocal weights are a reasonable choice—for, if the variance of an estimate is big, the weight should be small; if the variance of the estimate is small, then the estimate should have a relatively heavy weight and count for more because we have that estimate more precisely pinned down. Weighting by reciprocal variances gives, under ideal circumstances, the most precise combination. For the

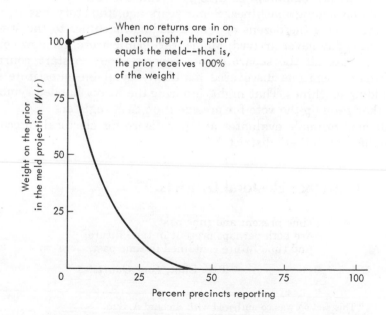

FIGURE 2-6 Weighting the prior in the overall meld

realities of election night, less simple combinations may be important. At any rate, one possible meld is the weighted average (weighted by the reciprocal of the variances) of the component projections:

$$\text{meld projection} = \frac{\dfrac{1}{S_c^2}\,\%D_c + \dfrac{1}{S_k^2}\,\%D_k + \dfrac{1}{w(r)}\,\%D_p}{\dfrac{1}{S_c^2} + \dfrac{1}{S_k^2} + \dfrac{1}{w(r)}}$$

where S_c^2 and S_k^2 are the variances of the estimates of $\%D_c$ and $\%D_k$. This is simply the particular realization of the general formula for a weighted average:

$$\text{weighted average} = \frac{\text{sum of weighted components}}{\text{sum of weights}} = \frac{\Sigma\, w_i x_i}{\Sigma\, w_i}.$$

Although based on the principles we have looked at here, contemporary projection models include many additional complications—complex estimation procedures, specially tailored base values, checks for bad data, and estimates of turnout. While today's elaborate models must be entirely computer based, in past years the votes were tabulated by hand on adding machines. Some years ago, the story has it, the truck delivering the dozens of rented adding machines to the studio on election day never arrived. Momentary panic arose, for how could they tabulate all the separate vote reports about to start pouring in? Finally, someone discovered a quickly available substitute for the adding machines. That night, ignoring the heavy-handed symbolism, they rang up the vote for president on cash registers

Our next example evaluates another device for electoral forecasting—the "bellwether" district.

Bellwether Electoral Districts[10]

> Time present and time past
> Are both perhaps present in time future,
> And time future contained in time past.
>
> —T. S. Eliot, *Four Quartets**

[10] This section was co-authored with Richard A. Sun.
    *From *Four Quartets* by T. S. Eliot. Reprinted by permission of the publishers, Harcourt Brace Jovanovich, Inc. and Faber and Faber Ltd.

Prior to the 1936 presidential election, the conventional political wisdom had it that as Maine voted, so went the rest of the nation. After the 46-state landslide, James Farley, Roosevelt's campaign manager, revised the theory: "As goes Maine, so goes Vermont." Such is perhaps the inevitable fate of so-called bellwether or barometric electoral districts; still, there are always new contenders with markedly unblemished records of retrospective accuracy to replace wayward bellwethers. Given the familiar inferential caution that retrospective accuracy provides little guarantee of prospective accuracy, what is the worth of claims that certain districts invariably reflect the national division of the vote?

The answers at hand differ: a skeptical statistician probably has little faith in the after-the-fact predictive success of bellwether districts; the collector of political folklore marvels at the record of such byways as Palo Alto County (Iowa) and Crook County, (Oregon) which have voted for the winner of every presidential election in this century; the newspaper reporter interviews a few citizens of Palo Alto or Crook County in search of "clues as to what will happen next Tuesday"; and Louis Bean has written four books premised on the notion that as goes X, so goes the country.[11] Here we will examine the question more deeply—and, at the same time, see a number of fundamental statistical techniques in action.

The data for the analysis are the election returns from almost all 3100 U.S. counties for the fourteen presidential elections from 1916 to 1968.[12] We will be looking for what are called "all-or-nothing" bellwethers: the county either votes for the winner of the presidential election or it does not. This seems to be the usual meaning of "bellwether district"; most discussions of supposed bellwethers report that the district has voted with the winner in the last N elections. Sometimes

[11] *Ballot Behavior* (Washington, D.C.: Public Affairs Press, 1940); *How to Predict Elections* (New York; Knopf, 1948) *How America Votes in Presidential Elections* (Metuchen, N.J.: Scarecrow Press, 1968); and *How to Predict the 1972 Election* (New York: Quadrangle, 1972).

[12] The data tapes were made available through the Inter-University Consortium for Political Research. We edited them extensively, correcting errors and adding missing data. Of the 3070 counties in the United States, we have the complete two-party election returns for the fourteen elections from 1916 to 1968 for 2938 counties, or 96 percent. The remaining counties had to be dropped because one election in the fourteen election series was missing; others may have changed names or are mixed in with other political units. A listing of the missing counties and election years was reviewed both before and after our analysis; both times it appears that the small amount of missing data had no consequences for our findings. Some of our early computations carried along votes for four different parties in each county, but we finally edited the data to include only the returns for the two major parties. Therefore all election returns reported here are based on the votes of the two major parties in all the elections.

N is surprisingly small; some journalists have interviewed nonrandomly selected citizens of "bellwether" communities that have voted for the winner in only three or four previous elections.

One good test of the credibility of bellwethers is to conduct a series of historical experiments, each designed to answer the question: How well would we have done in predicting the election of 19XX if we had followed a group of supposedly bellwether counties chosen on the basis of past elections before the election of 19XX? For example, going into the 1968 election, there were 49 counties that had voted for the winner in every presidential election since 1916—thirteen elections (or more) in a row with the winner. Were these 49 retrospective bellwethers more likely than other counties to support the winner in 1968? This is the sort of question that we will answer over and over, for different elections and for different choices of historical bellwethers.

Since they directly answer the question at hand, the historical experiments seem to provide the most powerful means of assessing the credibility of bellwethers. It is also possible to construct probability models to provide a baseline or null hypothesis against which to compare the observed performance of reputed bellwethers. We met with little success in developing models based on reasonable assumptions. The construction of a useful probability model remains an open question, although we suspect that even a very good model would still not provide as direct and powerful test of bellwethers as the historical experiment.

Another statistical problem arises because bellwethers are found in an after-the-fact search through election returns; there is no theory identifying particular areas as potential bellwethers before the fact. We have then a situation analogous to that of "shotgunning" in survey research: the searching through of a large body of data for statistically significant results leads to difficulties in just how to include the fact of the search in an adjusted significance test. One answer is simply the independent replication on a fresh collection of data of the results found through searching. That is, of course, the underlying logic of the historical experiment: bellwethers are chosen from a search, and then we see if their bellwether performance is replicated in the historical future.

The usual technique for evaluating bellwethers is retrospective admiration of the historical record. Almost all written accounts of reputed bellwethers describe an area's lengthy record in voting for winners and then ask, in effect, "Isn't that something?" These accounts evaluate the predictive performance of the past without reference to either prospective accuracy or the predictive record of other areas. Consider excerpts from a typical *New York Times* story on bellwethers:

Town Votes 'Em As It Sees 'Em
And It Usually Sees 'Em Right

Salem, N.J., April 8—The political professionals are keeping an
eye on this small Quaker community in southern New Jersey for
clues to the outcome of the presidential election.

For fifty years, with only two exceptions, Salem has voted for
the victorious Presidential candidate. . . .

There is no clear reason for Salem's stature as an election indicator.

"But," says County Clerk Thomas J. Grieves, "you can't call it
chance or a quirk. It happens too often. . . ."[13]

Actually, there are several hundred counties with predictive records
better than Salem's over the last fifty years. But the important point
is that no evaluation of Salem's record can be made on the basis
of past election returns from Salem alone. A bellwether's credibility
can only be assessed by examining, in comparison to other districts,
its *predictive* record and not merely its postdictive record.

Consider the following historical experiment: let us choose the
counties with the best records for predicting presidential elections
from 1916 to 1964 and see how well they predicted the outcome of
the 1968 election. There were 49 such counties with records of
supporting the winner in all 13 elections from 1916 to 1964. Such
a record, by almost any standard, is a bellwether performance—*if*
the counties had been identified in 1916 instead of after the fact.
How well did the 49 retrospective bellwethers of 1916–1964 do in
predicting the winner in 1968? Not very well at all; 27 of the 49
(or 55.1 percent) voted with the winner in 1968. Two-thirds of *all*
counties supported the winner in 1968, and so a county chosen at
random could typically have been expected to outpredict the counties
with previously perfect predictive records. Table 2-3 shows the full
array of results, with the 1968 predictive performance tabulated
against the prior record of predictive accuracy. Oddly enough, the
best predictions in 1968 were made by counties that had had the
worst record in the past (5 right, 8 wrong). These 80 counties (that
went 100 percent for the winner in 1968) were, of course, counties
that had voted without fail for the Republican candidate in every
previous election since 1916 and persisted in 1968. So it is easy to
find a group of counties, identified by their past voting record, that
will support the upcoming winner—if you only know how the election
is going to turn out!

The election of 1968 was a particularly bad year for the bellwethers
of the past. Table 2-4, repeating the tests for the presidential elections
from 1936 to 1964, shows that for some elections the bellwethers

[13] *The New York Times*, April 9, 1964, p. 29.

TABLE 2-3

Predictive Performance from 1916 to 1964 Compared with Predictive Record
in 1968 Election

Past Performance, 1916–1964				1968 Performance			
Past Predictions		Counties		Right		Wrong	
Right	Wrong	Number	Percent	Number	Percent	Number	Per-cent
0	13	0	0.0	0	0.0	0	0.0
1	12	0	0.0	0	0.0	0	0.0
2	11	0	0.0	0	0.0	0	0.0
3	10	0	0.0	0	0.0	0	0.0
4	9	0	0.0	0	0.0	0	0.0
5	8	80	2.7	80	100.0	0	0.0
6	7	229	7.8	209	91.3	20	8.7
7	6	502	17.1	303	60.3	199	39.6
8	5	708	24.1	424	59.9	284	40.1
9	4	554	18.8	397	71.6	157	28.3
10	3	380	12.9	251	66.0	129	33.9
11	2	274	9.3	148	54.0	126	45.9
12	1	162	5.5	97	59.9	65	40.1
13	0	49	1.6	27	55.1	22	44.9
		2938	100.0	1936	65.9	1002	34.1

of the past do predict the upcoming election somewhat more accurately
than a typical county.

Tables 2-3 and 2-4 provide us with a great deal of experience with
retrospective all-or-nothing bellwethers. The tables suggest:

1. Perhaps each time one hears of an area with a spectacular
predictive record in the past, a glimmer of hope and curiosity arises
suggesting that surely this fine record couldn't be mere chance—there
must be *something* going on. Whatever that something might be,
it isn't a high degree of prospective accuracy. Sometimes previously
accurate districts do better than just any collection of districts;
sometimes they don't. The retrospective bellwethers were particularly
poor in the close elections of 1960 and 1968. The compilations of
Table 2-4 show the erratic record of the retrospective all-or-nothing
bellwethers in predicting the future.

2. We have identified "bellwethers" in Tables 2-3 and 2-4 by their
previously perfect predictive records in at least six consecutive previous
elections. If this standard is applied to judging the results of our
historical experiment, then the bellwethers of the past are not the
bellwethers of the present. In five of the eight elections, the previously
bellwether counties had a higher probability of voting with the winner

TABLE 2-4
Predictive Record of Previously Accurate Counties in Presidential Elections,
1940–1964

PREDICTING 1940	Number of counties	Percent voting with winner, 1940
1916–1936 past performance, right-wrong = 6-0	602	52.9
Nationwide	2938	61.6

PREDICTING 1944	Number of counties	Percent voting with winner, 1944
1916–1940 past performance, right-wrong = 7-0	319	72.7
Nationwide	2938	55.3

PREDICTING 1948	Number of counties	Percent voting with winner, 1948
1916–1944 past performance, right-wrong = 8-0	232	87.5
Nationwide	2938	59.9

PREDICTING 1952	Number of counties	Percent voting with winner, 1952
1916–1948 past performance, right-wrong = 9-0	203	81.3
Nationwide	2938	68.3

PREDICTING 1956	Number of counties	Percent voting with winner, 1956
1916–1952 past performance, right-wrong = 10-0	165	87.3
Nationwide	2938	70.0

PREDICTING 1960	Number of counties	Percent voting with winner, 1960
1916–1956 past performance, right-wrong = 11-0	144	35.4
Nationwide	2938	38.6

PREDICTING 1964	Number of counties	Percent voting with winner, 1964
1916–1960 past performance, right-wrong = 12-0	51	96.1
Nationwide	2938	73.3

than a county chosen at random from the nation as a whole; in the other three elections (1940, 1960, and 1968), a county chosen at random would be the county of choice in predicting the upcoming election.

3. The retrospective bellwethers, *taken as a group,* correctly predicted seven of the eight trial elections—in the sense that a majority of the group of retrospective bellwethers supported the winner. Exactly the same was true of a group of randomly selected counties (within the limits of sampling error).

4. There were, alas, no anti-bellwether counties. No county had such an outstandingly poor record that it could serve, by reversing its preferences, as a predictive (or even postdictive) guide.

5. Tables 2-3 and 2-4 indicate clearly why one obvious probability model, the binomial, for all-or-nothing bellwethers does not provide a useful baseline. Consider the following: if a fair coin, labeled "Democratic candidate will win" on one side and "Republican candidate will win" on the other, were tossed prior to each of the last 14 presidential elections, the probability that the coin would successfully predict the winner of all 14 contests is

$$\left(\frac{1}{2}\right)^{14} = \frac{1}{16,384} = .000061.$$

If this toss of the coin were performed in each of the 3100 counties, then it would be expected that

$$(.000061)\ (3100) = 0.2 \text{ counties}$$

would correctly go along with the winner 14 elections in a row. More generally, the binomial model for k successes in 14 independent trials with probability of success equal to one-half generates the distribution of predictions shown in Figure 2-7. The actual distribution of counties is also shown in the figure. It is clear that the distribution of actual election outcomes is not generated by a process of 14 independent trials with probability of success equal to one-half. That is because the probability of success usually substantially exceeds one-half and the trials are, in fact, highly dependent. The chances that a given county votes with the winner is usually around two-thirds, as Tables 2-3 and 2-4 show.

A more difficult problem in constructing a probability model is that the election results are not independent over space and time: both the interelection and intercounty correlations are very high. For example, the correlation between the division of the vote from one election to the next over all counties is almost always greater

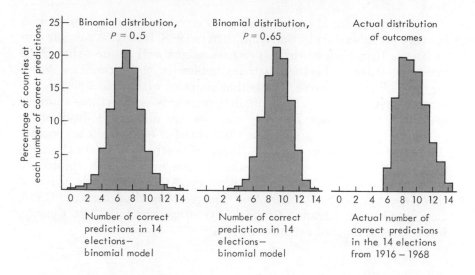

FIGURE 2-7   Binomial and actual outcome distributions

than .90. Considering that a county could go either Democratic or Republican in each of the 14 elections yields $2^{14} = 16,384$ theoretically possible electoral histories or paths that the counties could have followed over the 56 years. Less than 400 of these electoral histories actually occur, and only about 30 contain more than a handful of counties. At least 40 percent of all counties have gone more or less straight Democratic or straight Republican with occasional deviations in landslide years (Table 2-5).

TABLE 2-5
Most Frequently Occurring County Electoral Histories, 1916–1968

History	Number of counties
Straight Democratic	200
Democratic, except 1964	160
Democratic, except 1968	54
Democratic, except 1964 and 1968	58
Straight Republican	79
Republican, except 1964	128
Republican, except 1932, 1936, and 1964	136
Republican, except 1916, 1932, 1936, and 1964	155
Followed nation, all elections	27
Followed nation, except 1960	68

6. Twenty-seven of the nation's 3100 counties voted for the winner in every presidential election from 1916 to 1968. It may be possible—or at least a firm believer in bellwethers might well argue—that there are some truly bellwether districts hidden in those counties. What we have shown, of course, is only that counties with perfect postdictive records have undistinguished predictive records—when those counties are *taken as a group.* The only way we can identify bellwethers is as members of such a group. One final shred of evidence is to consider the performance of the nation's finest bellwethers. Prior to the 1960 election, there were eight counties in the nation with records of supporting every winner in this century. After 1968, only three of these eight superbellwethers still had unblemished records: Crook County, Oregon; Laramie County, Wyoming; and Palo Alto County, Iowa. They remained accurate in 1972.

Our conclusion in the case of all-or-nothing bellwethers is clear: the usual concept of a bellwether electoral district has no useful predictive properties. The all-or-nothing counties are only a curiosity and probably should be forgotten. It is a waste of time to send reporters out to interview nonrandomly selected citizens of Crook County a week or two before the election—at least it is a waste of time from any sort of scientific point of view. Such news reports create mystery where little exists.

There perhaps remains a magical air about the bellwethers of the past; some of these districts, considered individually, seemingly have such phenomenal records and yet we know better than to take them seriously—but still. . . . It may be best to look not to the election returns for the source of the mystery, but rather to ourselves. Maugham once wrote:

> The faculty for myth is innate in the human race. It seizes with avidity upon any incidents, surprising or mysterious, in the career of those who have distinguished themselves from their fellows, and invents a legend to which it then attaches a fanatical belief. It is the protest of romance against the commonplace of life. [14]

[14] Somerset Maugham, *The Moon and Sixpence* (Harmondsworth, Middlesex, England: Penguin Books, 1941), p. 7.

Regression Toward the Mean: How Prior Selection Affects the Measurement of Future Performance

Consider the defects in research design in the following example:

> Students in a statistics course who needed remedial teaching (as indicated by their performance in the lower quartile of an achievement test in arithmetic) were assigned to a special class in sensitivity training. Soon the teacher of the special class was able to go into full-time educational consulting because of the success of his new book, *Ending Educational Hangups in Statistics: How Empathy Pays Off*. The book showed that the special class was strikingly effective because when the students in the special class took the tests again after only six months, their test scores had greatly increased—increased, in fact, almost all the way up to the average of the first test scores of all the students who initially took the arithmetic test.

Several difficulties that are common in research designs compromise this hypothetical example.

This design uses the first test to divide the class into a treatment group (consisting of the lower quartile of students) and a control group (the remainder of the class). Students in the treatment group took the same tests again six months after joining the special class. The following comparisons were made in an effort to assess the benefits of the special class:

1. Average "gain" for special class equals

$$
\left(\begin{array}{l} \text{average of scores on} \\ \text{second test for special} \\ \text{class} \end{array} \right) \quad \text{minus} \quad \left(\begin{array}{l} \text{average of scores on} \\ \text{first test for special} \\ \text{class} \end{array} \right)
$$

2. "Improvement" relative to rest of class equals

$$
\left(\begin{array}{l} \text{average of scores on} \\ \text{second test for special} \\ \text{group} \end{array} \right) \quad \text{minus} \quad \left(\begin{array}{l} \text{average of scores for} \\ \text{whole class on the first} \\ \text{test} \end{array} \right)
$$

Two serious defects in the research design result in a bias in the "gain" and "improvement" scores such that the beneficial effect of the special class is exaggerated. The first defect is the failure to take into account the effect of practice and maturation on the test scores. Students taking a test a second time, as in the special class, can be generally expected to get better at taking tests; consequently, their scores improve merely because of their increased experience. Similarly, since the treatment-group scores on the second test are compared with the earlier test scores of the control group, a bias due to the maturation of the special group results. In other words, the students in the special group may improve relative to their previous performance (and the previous performance of their contemporaries) merely because they are older and smarter and not because they are necessarily benefiting from the special class.

In this design, then, the improvements in the scores of the special group due to practice and maturation effects are incorrectly attributed to the effect of the special class. Although it is impossible without additional information (or a better research design—see below) to judge the exact strength of the bias, we do at least know its direction: it favors the hypothesis that there is benefit from the special class.

The second defect in the research design is more subtle. It is a version of what is called the "regression fallacy." If members of a group are selected because their scores are extreme (either high or low) on a variable and if this extreme group are later tested once again, we will generally find that the group are "more average" than they were on the first test. Their scores will have moved or "regressed" toward the mean. One way to view the situation is to think of the extreme group as consisting of two sorts of people: (a) those who deserve really to be in that group and (b) those who are there because of random error—unlucky guesses on the test, an "off" day, and so forth. When the extreme group is tested a second time, the group (b) will typically perform more like their true selves, thereby raising their scores on the average at least. The deserving extremists in group (a) will continue their poor scores, albeit with some variation.

Thus the average score of the extreme group will typically increase because of the more typical performance of group (b) on the second test. There is no way of distinguishing group (a) from group (b) with only one test.

The problem arises when any group is formed by selecting its members because they are extreme on a single measure. For example, let us say that the highest quartile of students were placed in the special class instead of the bottom quartile. What would happen then? Once again, two types of students make up the extreme top group:

(a) those who are actually skilled and who deserve to be placed in the top quartile and (b) those who are lucky, who guess right, and so on. Now if this group is tested once again, it will generally be found that the overall average of the original extreme group has dropped somewhat—because not all the lucky performers on the first test will be lucky again.

The fallacy occurs in all sorts of situations. Wallis and Roberts provide several good examples including the following:

> Teachers—except, of course, statistics teachers—sometimes commit the regression fallacy in comparing grades on a final examination with those on a midterm examination. They find that their competent teaching has succeeded, on the average, in improving the performance of those who had seemed at midterm to be in precarious condition. This accomplishment naturally brings the teacher keen satisfaction, which is only partially dampened by the fact that the best students at midterm have done somewhat less on the final—an "obvious" indication of slackening off by these students due to overconfidence. [15]

Let us examine a numerical example of what might have happened in the case of the special class. Make the following assumptions:

1. There are no practice or maturation effects.
2. The special class has no effect at all on the students' test scores.

Under these assumptions we should observe no significant gains or improvements by the special class if the research design is free of bias. If, however, the research design has a bias, we will be able to get at least an approximate idea of its extent. Table 2-6 shows three sets of made-up test scores:

Column I: *The "true score" of each student on the test.* This, of course, is never actually measured perfectly, and the remaining columns represent the true score plus some random measurement error.

Column II: *The "true score" for each student with a random number between −20 and 20 added to each score.*

Column III: *Again the "true score" with another random number added to column I.*

Let the numbers in column II represent the scores of all the students on the first test and those in column III the scores on the second test. Since the test scores were computed by adding a random error to the "true scores," we find that there is very little difference in

[15] W. Allen Wallis and Harry V. Roberts, *Statistics: A New Approach* (New York: Free Press, 1956), p. 262.

TABLE 2-6
Random Errors Added to True Scores

	I		II		III
		Random	Observed	Random	Observed
	True	error,	score,	error,	score,
Student	score	test 1	test 1	test 2	test 2
A	70	+13	83*	+1	71
B	75	−20	55*	+15	90
C	80	+8	88	−13	67
D	84	+7	91	−1	83
E	87	−15	72*	−9	78
F	90	+2	92	+8	98
G	93	−4	89	+12	105
H	95	−7	88	+16	111
I	96	+3	99	−12	84
J	97	+17	114	+20	117
K	98	−19	79*	−1	97
L	99	+11	110	+5	104
M	99	−18	81*	−17	82
N	100	−13	87*	+3	103
O	100	+9	109	−7	93
P	101	+12	113	+10	111
Q	101	−0	101	−5	96
R	102	−18	84*	+2	104
S	103	+13	116	+9	112
T	104	+7	111	−15	89
U	105	+3	108	+14	119
V	107	+12	119	−7	100
W	110	−11	99	+16	126
X	113	−20	93	+5	118
Y	116	+15	131	−19	97
Z	120	+1	121	+5	125
AA	125	−2	123	−2	123
BB	130	−14	116	−14	116

*The asterisk indicates students in lowest quartile on test 1.

the average score of the whole class on test 1 compared with test 2. Also the test seems to be measuring something: the correlation between the tests is .51. The correlation would be perfect, if we had not introduced the random measurement error into the true score on each test. Furthermore, note that the variability on both tests 1 and 2 is the same.

It should be clear that all that has been done is to construct some test scores containing some random error. No systematic effects in the data enable one to differentiate between the results of test 1 and test 2. But let us now see what happens in the research design used in assessing the effects of the special class. The students in the special class were chosen because they were in the bottom of the class on the first test. Compare, then, the scores of the lowest seven students in the class as measured by test 1 (Table 2-7).

This research design generates the following misleading results. The average score of the group entering the special class was 77.3; after attending the special class for six months, their average score was 89.3—a "gain" of 12.0 points. Thus, because of the regression effects operating in this research design, a *pseudo-gain of 12 points* was found between test 1 and test 2, even though all the difference between test 1 and test 2 was generated by random numbers.

Note how plausible it all seems. A group of students are selected on the basis of test scores to enter the special class, and when the same students are tested later, those in the special class appear to have gained 12 points. Test 1 and test 2 are rather highly correlated, indicating that the tests are moderately reliable. And yet it is all a statistical artifact.

What would be a better research design—one that assesses the effect, if any, of the special class but avoids the bias resulting from the effects of practice, maturation, and regression toward the mean? The essential feature of an improved research designs is that not all of the low scorers should be placed in the special group. Ideally, some of the low scorers on test 1 should be randomly assigned to the special group; the others should remain in the regular class. In evaluating the effects of the special class, then, the basic comparison should be made between those low scorers in special class versus those low scorers in the regular class. Regression toward the mean still operates in this design, but its impact is roughly equal on the

TABLE 2-7

Scores on Test 1 Compared to Scores on Test 2 for the Lowest Quartile of Students on Test 1: Pseudo-Gains and Pseudo-Losses

Student	Test 1	Test 2	Difference: "Gain" > 0 "Loss" < 0
A	83	71	−12
B	55	90	35
E	72	78	6
K	79	97	18
M	81	82	1
N	87	103	13
R	84	104	20

control group and the treatment group because students were randomly assigned to the two groups.

The improved design, however, does give us a chance to separate out the genuine effects resulting from membership in the special class from the artifactual effects deriving from practice, maturation, and regression toward the mean. The original design confounds these factors and throws them all into the gain score.

This example also illustrates the utility of trying out the design and analysis on realistic but random data. Random data contain no substantive effects; thus if the analysis of the random data results in some sort of effect, then we know that the analysis is producing that spurious effect, and we must be on the lookout for such artifacts when the genuine data are analyzed.

Prediction of Accident Proneness:
Can Producers of Automobile Accidents
Be Identified in Advance as
Consumers of Traffic Violations?

Only a small number of drivers are involved in severe automobile accidents. This fact gives rise to statements like "Three percent of all drivers produce one hundred percent of all severe accidents." The statement, while true, can be misleading. It does not mean that a small group of drivers go around systematically running down people or ramming other cars. "Accident proneness" may or may not be a useful concept.

It is empirically true that a small number of people, not necessarily identifiable in advance, are involved in serious accidents. Do these people have any characteristics in common? Can we ascertain roughly the probability that a given driver will be involved in an accident within a certain period of time? Insurance companies already make such predictions in a crude way by setting their rates in relation to factors including the driver's age, sex, marital status, accident history, type of driving, and record of traffic violations. Such procedures, at least as they are employed in Canada, are biased against some drivers (particularly high-risk drivers) because the various factors are not independent, resulting in double counting of risks against some drivers.[16]

[16] See R. A. Holmes, "Discriminatory Bias in Rates Charged by the Canadian Automobile Insurance Industry," *Journal of the American Statistical Association*, 65 (March 1970), 108–22.

A study of the relationship between the number of traffic violations a driver collects and his or her involvement in accidents is threatened by possible spurious correlations. First, one result of a motor vehicle accident is a traffic ticket. One driver or another is found to have committed a violation which "explains" the accident. This leads to statements such as "Accidents are caused by excessive speed," which are based on evidence that in many accidents, drivers involved are adjudged to have exceeded the speed limit. Lacking here is a comparison group of the speed of drivers *not* involved in accidents. There is some evidence that a large proportion of all drivers on the road are, in fact, exceeding the speed limit. In any case, a first step in a study of traffic violations and accidents is to control for the tickets produced by accidents—at least if the task is to predict, on the basis of a past history of traffic violations, that certain drivers will be more likely to be involved in accidents.

A second problem of potential spuriousness is suggested by the following model:

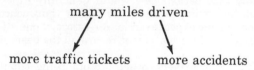

Thus, high-mileage drivers face greater exposure to the risk of both a traffic ticket and an accident—even if they drive with a care equal to that of low-mileage drivers.

A review of the studies of the relationship between violations and accident involvements points to both of these problems and to a partial solution:

> Ross investigated the relationship between violations and accidents for the 36 accident-involved drivers . . . and found that 12 of these 36 drivers had reported traffic convictions on their official records. These 12 people had 18 convictions. However, since there was no control group in this study, it is not possible to ascertain whether drivers with accidents had a higher violation rate than drivers without accidents. A point made by Ross, and one which has an important bearing on other studies using official records or information collected in interviews, is that there were discrepancies between interviewee-reported and recorded accidents and violations large enough to throw question upon studies relying on one or the other source of information in arriving at an accident or violation record.
>
> As part of a California driver record study, relationships between concurrent recorded accidents and citations (convictions for moving traffic violations) were analyzed. The data for this analysis consisted of a random sample of 225,000 out of approximately eleven million existing California driving records. Each driving record included a three-year history of both accidents and citations. To avoid inadvertent

correlation effects, citations directly resulting from accident investigations were labeled as "spurious" and were removed from the citation counts in most of the analysis.

The driver records were grouped according to the number of nonspurious citations, and the mean number of accidents per 100 drivers was calculated for each group. This analysis indicated an approximately linear relationship between citations and accidents with fluctuations at the high end of the citation count scale as a result of reduced sample size. Whereas those with no countable citations in the three-year period had only 14 accidents per 100 individuals, those with five citations had 62 accidents per 100 individuals and those with nine or more citations had 89 accidents per 100 individuals.

These figures indicate that there is a strong relationship between the mean number of accidents per driver and the number of concurrent citations when large groups of drivers are considered. On the other hand, the correlation coefficient between accidents and nonspurious citations was only 0.23. This low figure indicates that large errors could be made if one attempted to estimate the number of accidents an individual driver had on the basis of his citation record over the same time period. One would generally expect the correlation between concurrent events to be higher than nonconcurrent events. Thus, one should expect even larger errors, if one attempted to predict an individual's future accident record on the basis of his past citation record.

High-mileage drivers, other factors being equal, are exposed to a higher risk of both accidents and citations. Variations from driver to driver in exposure in general and annual mileage in particular may produce part of the correlation between accidents and citations that has been observed. Another California study examined characteristics of negligent drivers, defined as those whose record indicated a point count of four or more in 12 months, of six or more in 24 months, or eight or more in 36 months. (A point is scored for each traffic violation involving the unsafe operation of a motor vehicle or accident for which the operator is deemed responsible; two points are scored for a few types of violations deemed especially serious.)

When the annual mileage for a group of negligent drivers over age 20 was compared with that for a random sample of renewal applicants it was found that the negligent group averaged 17,219 miles per year while the applicant group averaged 7,449 miles per year. When males and females were treated separately it was found that negligent males averaged 17,591 miles per year as contrasted to 9,649 miles per year for the male applicants, while negligent females averaged 9,403 miles per year as contrasted to 5,519 miles per year for female applicants. The negligent drivers may have inflated their reported annual mileage in order to impress officials with their need to drive; nevertheless, it appears very likely that the negligent drivers do indeed drive more than average.[17]

[17] The State of the Art of Traffic Safety, by Arthur D. Little, Inc., for the Automobile Manufacturers Association, Inc. (Cambridge, Mass.: Arthur D. Little, Inc., June 1966) pp. 42–43.

Spellbinding Extrapolation

One of the most spellbinding efforts at simple extrapolation beyond the data arises in this history of guano:

> Guano, as most people understand, is imported from the [islands of the] Pacific—mostly of the Chincha group, off the coast of Peru, and under the dominion of that government.
>
> Its sale is made a monopoly, and the avails, to a great extent, go to pay the British holders of Peruvian Government bonds, giving them, to all intents and purposes, a lien upon the profits of a treasure intrinsically more valuable than the gold mines of California. There are deposits of this unsurpassed fertilizer, in some places, to the depth of sixty or seventy feet, and over large extents of surface. The guano fields are generally conceded to be the excrements of aquatic fowls, which live and nestle in great numbers around the islands. They seem designed by nature to rescue, at least in part, that untold amount of fertilizing material which every river and brooklet is rolling into the sea. The wash of alluvial soils, the floating refuse of the field and forest, and, above all, the wasted materials of great cities, are constantly being carried by the tidal currents out to sea. These, to a certain extent at least, go to nourish, directly or indirectly, submarine vegetable and animal life, which in turn goes to feed the birds, whose excrements in our day are brought away by the ship-load from the Chincha Islands.
>
> The bird is a beautifully arranged chemical laboratory, fitted up to perform a single operation, viz.: to take the fish as food, burn out the carbon by means of its respiratory functions, and deposit the remainder in the shape of an incomparable fertilizer. But how many ages have these depositions of seventy feet in thickness been accumulating!
>
> There are at the present day countless numbers of the birds resting upon the islands at night; but, according to Baron Humboldt, the excrements of the birds for the space of three centuries would not form a stratum over one-third of an inch in thickness. By an easy mathematical calculation, it will be seen, that at this rate of deposition, it would take seven thousand five hundred and sixty centuries, or seven hundred and fifty-six thousand years, to form the deepest guano bed. Such a calculation carries us back well on towards a former geological period, and proves one, and perhaps both, of two things—first, that in past ages, an infinitely greater number of these birds hovered over the islands; and secondly, that the material world existed at a period long anterior to its fitness as the abode of man. The length of man's existence is infinitesimal, compared with such a cycle of years; and the facts recorded on every leaf of the material universe ought, if it does not, to teach us humility. That a little

bird, whose individual existence is as nothing, should, in its united action, produce the means of bringing back to an active fertility whole provinces of waste and barren lands, is one of a thousand facts to show how comparatively insignificant agencies in the economy of nature produce momentous results.[18]

Rather substantial inferences, given the observed data!

[18] *London Farmer's Magazine: Prospectus of the American Guano Company* (New York: John F. Trow, 1855).

CHAPTER 3

Two-Variable Linear Regression

"Yet to calculate is not in itself to analyze."

—Edgar Allen Poe, *The Murders in the Rue Morgue*

Introduction

Fitting lines to relationships between variables is the major tool of data analysis. Fitted lines often effectively summarize the data and, by doing so, help communicate the analytic results to others. Estimating a fitted line is also the first step in squeezing further information from the data. Since the observed value can be broken up into two pieces,

observation = fitted value + residual,

we can therefore find the remaining part of the observed value that is unexplained,

residual = observation − fitted value,

and work with the residuals to discover a more complete explanation of the influences on the response variable.[1] Such was the procedure used in the study of automobile safety inspections in Chapter 1.

[1] This follows J. W. Tukey and M. B. Wilk, "Data Analysis and Statistics: Techniques and Approaches," in E. R. Tufte, ed., *The Quantitative Analysis of Social Problems* (Reading, Mass.: Addison-Wesley, 1970), pp. 373–74.

We now briefly review the mechanics of linear regression. The equation of a straight line is

$$Y = \beta_0 + \beta_1 X,$$

where β_0 is the intercept and β_1 is the slope as shown in Figure 3-1. The observed data are used to estimate the two parameters, β_0 and β_1, of the model. The actual numerical *estimates* of the intercept and the slope are written as $\hat{\beta}_0$ and $\hat{\beta}_1$, where the "hats" indicate that the quantity is an estimate of a model parameter—an estimate that is computed from the observed data.

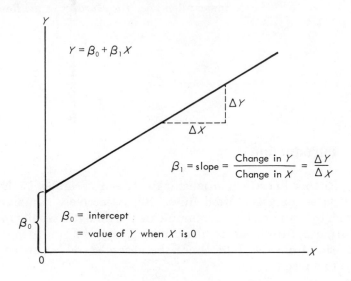

FIGURE 3-1   Equation of a straight line

The slope, a summary of the relationship between X and Y, answers the question: when X changes by one unit, by how many units does Y change? The answer is that Y changes by β_1 units. Consider the following example. In the 36 congressional elections from 1900 to 1972, the line (shown in Figure 3-2)

$$\% \text{ seats Democratic} = -49.64 + 2.07 \; (\% \text{ votes Democratic})$$

fits the relationship between the share of congressional seats won by the Democrats and the share of votes that party received nationwide for their congressional candidates. The estimated slope, $\hat{\beta}_1$, is 2.07; that is,

$$\hat{\beta}_1 = \frac{\text{change in } Y}{\text{change in } X} = \frac{\text{change in percent of seats}}{\text{change in percent of votes}} = 2.07.$$

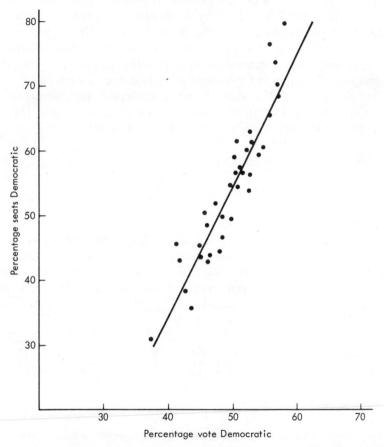

Percentage seats Democratic = −49.64 + 2.07 (Percentage votes Democratic)

$$Y = -49.64 + 2.07X$$

N = 37 Congressional elections, 1900–1972

FIGURE 3-2 Fitted line and observed data

This means that a one percent change in the share of the Democratic vote was typically accompanied by a change of 2.07 percent in the Democratic share of seats in Congress. Thus an increase of only one percent in the share of the vote was worth a substantially larger increase (of a little over two percent) in the share of seats. Of course, it works the other way, too: a drop of one percent of the vote is associated with a loss of two percent of seats. Figure 3-2 shows the data and the fitted line. In this *particular* case, the estimate of the slope measures what is called the "swing ratio"—the swing or change in seats for a given change in votes. Often, then, the substance of the problem gives a special meaning to the slope, even though the mechanics of computing the slope are the same in each case.

The estimates of the slope and the intercept are chosen so as to minimize the sum of the squares of the residuals from the fitted line. This is the principle of *least squares,* which says

$$\text{minimize } \Sigma \, e_i^2,$$

—that is, minimize $\Sigma \, (Y_i - \hat{Y}_i)^2$

in the notation of Figure 3-3.

One of the glories of the principle of least squares is that it leads immediately to specific instructions as to how to use the data to compute $\hat{\beta}_0$ and $\hat{\beta}_1$ such that they uniquely satisfy the principle. The mathematics are found in any statistics text, where it is proved that the least-squares estimates of the slope and the intercept are computed from the observed data by

$$\hat{\beta}_1 = \frac{\Sigma \, (X_i - \bar{X})(Y_i - \bar{Y})}{\Sigma \, (X_i - \bar{X})^2}$$

$$\hat{\beta}_0 = \bar{Y} - \hat{\beta}_1 \bar{X}.$$

The fitted line minimizes errors in prediction when X *is used to predict* Y—and the errors in prediction are measured with respect to the Y variable. The estimate of the slope in this case is the *slope of the regression of Y on X.* If the roles of X and Y were reversed, and the values of X predicted from the variable labeled Y, then we would be looking at the regression of X on Y. In this second case, the errors in prediction are measured with respect to the X axis. Unless all the observed points fall on a straight line, the two slopes are not equal. Thus the regression model is asymmetric—since the describing variable and the response variable are treated differently and different fitted lines result, depending upon which variable the researcher decides is the response variable and which is the describing variable.

Note that the question of a possible causal relationship is not decided by calling one variable the describing variable and the other the response variable. The question of causality is a separate and often difficult issue. By effectively summarizing the data, the regression

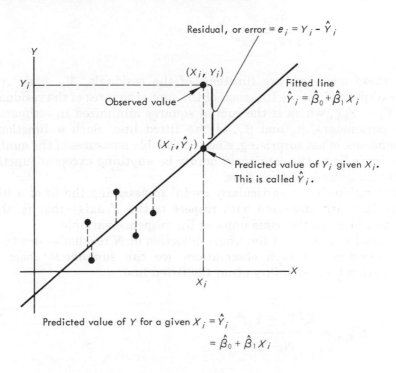

FIGURE 3-3   Notation for least-squares regression

analysis may sometimes provide some help in deciding if there is a causal relationship between the variables.

After fitting a line to a collection of data, the obvious question is: How well does the line fit? Here are four measures of the quality of fit:

1. the N residuals: $Y_i - \hat{Y}_i$,
2. the residual variation:

$$S^2_{Y|X} = \frac{\Sigma (Y_i - \hat{Y}_i)^2}{N - 2},$$

3. the ratio of explained to total variation:

$$r^2 = \frac{\Sigma\,(\hat{Y}_i - \bar{Y})^2}{\Sigma\,(Y_i - \bar{Y})^2},$$

4. the standard error of the estimate of the slope:

$$\frac{S_{Y|X}}{\sqrt{\Sigma\,(X_i - \bar{X})^2}}.$$

All these measures are functions of the residuals, $Y_i - \hat{Y}_i$. And all except the first are functions of the sum of squares of the residuals, $\Sigma\,(Y_i - \hat{Y}_i)^2$, which is the sum of squares minimized in estimating the parameters, β_0 and β_1, of the fitted line. Such a functional dependence is not surprising, since reasonable measures of the quality of a line's fit to the data could hardly be anything except a function of the magnitude of the errors.

The residuals are particularly useful in assessing the fit of a line, since they are measured with respect to the Y axis—that is, they are measured in the same units as the response variable.

Instead of looking at the whole collection of N residuals—for there is a residual for each observation—we can summarize them by estimating the variability about the fitted line:

$$S_{Y|X}^2 = \frac{\Sigma\,(Y_i - \hat{Y}_i)^2}{N - 2}.$$

Sometimes the square root is taken, yielding the residual standard error for the fitted line.

Probably the most frequently used measure assessing the quality of fit of the line is r^2, the proportion of the variance explained. Figure 3-4 shows the components of r^2. For a given observation, $Y_i - \bar{Y}$ is the deviation of that observation from the mean, $\bar{Y}$. And $\Sigma\,(Y_i - \bar{Y})^2$ is the total variation in Y (that is, the sum of the squares of all the deviations from the mean). The describing variable seeks to predict or explain the individual deviations from the mean. The error in prediction for the ith observation is $Y_i - \hat{Y}_i$; and the error variation for all the observations is $\Sigma\,(Y_i - \hat{Y}_i)^2$. An intuitively sensible measure of the fit of the line is the ratio of this error or

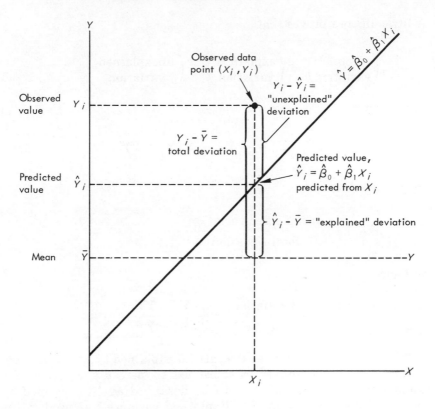

FIGURE 3-4   Components of Y^2

unexplained variation to the total variation; the smaller this ratio, the better the fit:

$$\text{one measure of fit}$$

$$= \frac{\text{unexplained variation in } Y}{\text{total variation in } Y}$$

$$= \frac{\Sigma (Y_i - \hat{Y}_i)^2}{\Sigma (Y_i - \bar{Y})^2}.$$

The commonly used measure, r^2, is simply this ratio subtracted from one:

$$r^2 = 1 - \frac{\Sigma (Y_i - \hat{Y}_i)^2}{\Sigma (Y_i - \bar{Y})^2}.$$

A little algebra proves that

$$\begin{pmatrix} \text{total} \\ \text{variation} \end{pmatrix} = \begin{pmatrix} \text{explained} \\ \text{variation} \end{pmatrix} + \begin{pmatrix} \text{unexplained} \\ \text{variation} \end{pmatrix}$$

or

$$\Sigma\,(Y_i - \bar{Y})^2 = \Sigma\,(\hat{Y}_i - \bar{Y})^2 + \Sigma\,(Y_i - \hat{Y})^2.$$

Therefore, since

$$r^2 = 1 - \frac{\text{unexplained variation}}{\text{total variation}}$$

we have

$$r^2 = \frac{\text{explained variation}}{\text{total variation}} = \frac{\Sigma\,(\hat{Y}_i - \bar{Y})^2}{\Sigma\,(Y_i - \bar{Y})^2}.$$

This interpretation of r^2, as the ratio of explained to total variation, is very common. Often r^2 is expressed in percentage terms—for example, a value of r^2 of .51 will be described as "X explained 51 percent of the variance in Y." "Explained variance," as used in the statistical jargon, refers only to the sum of squares, $\Sigma\,(\hat{Y}_i - \bar{Y})^2$. It may or may not refer to a good substantive explanation. A big r^2 means that X is relatively successful in predicting the value of Y— not necessarily that X causes Y or even that X is a meaningful explanation of Y. As you might imagine, some researchers, in presenting their results, tend to play on the ambiguity of the word "explain" in this context to avoid the risk of making an out-and-out assertion of causality while creating the appearance that something really was explained substantively as well as statistically.

If the fitted line has no errors of fit (that is, if the observed points all lie in a straight line), r^2 equals 1.00, since there is no unexplained variation. At the other extreme, if the describing variable is no help at all in predicting the value of Y, r^2 will be near zero, since no variance is explained. In this unfortunate case, the regression line is simply $\hat{Y} = \bar{Y}$ (in other words, the predicted value of Y does not depend on the value of X).

In evaluating the fitted line, it is useful to know if the slope differs from zero. If the slope does not differ meaningfully from zero, then

X gives no help in explaining Y—the line is $\hat{Y} = \bar{Y}$. As explained in textbooks on statistics, a test of statistical significance and a confidence interval for the estimate of slope is constructed from the standard error of the estimate of the slope, which equals

$$S_{\hat{\beta}_1} = \frac{S_{Y|X}}{\sqrt{\Sigma\,(X_i - \bar{X})^2}}.$$

To conduct the test of statistical significance for $\hat{\beta}_1 \neq 0$, we consider the ratio of the estimated slope and its standard error:

$$\frac{\hat{\beta}_1 - 0}{S_{\hat{\beta}_1}}.$$

Under appropriate statistical assumptions, this has a t-distribution, with $N - 2$ degrees of freedom. For N greater than 30, the t-distribution closely matches the normal distribution. It is this match that gives rise to the rule of thumb that a regression coefficient should be roughly twice its standard error if it is to be statistically significant at the .05 level—since, for the normal, the two-tailed .05 limits are at ± 1.96 standard deviations.

Finally, note from the denominator of the formula for $S_{\hat{\beta}_1}$ that the error in the estimate of the slope grows smaller as the variability of X increases; that is, if the observations on the X variable are spread out instead of bunched together, the standard error of the estimate of the slope will be reduced. Consequently, if there is reason to believe that there is a linear relation between X and Y and if we can control the intervals at which X is measured, then it is better to choose values of X over a fairly wide range rather than bunched up together. For example, in a study of the effects of class size on teaching effectiveness, it would be better to construct classes of size 10, 15, and 20 students rather than 13, 15, and 17. By doing so, we might obtain a more secure estimate of the relationship between size and effectiveness.

This section has outlined the statistical mechanics of two-variable linear regression. We now apply the methods to a variety of data.

Example 1: Presidential Popularity and the Results of Congressional Elections

Let us, by way of review, apply all the different statistics estimated in the linear regression model to a single problem. Figure

3-5 shows the relationship between the President's approval rating (from the Gallup Poll) shortly before the midterm congressional election and the number of seats the President's political party loses in that congressional election, from 1946 to 1970. Table 3-1 shows

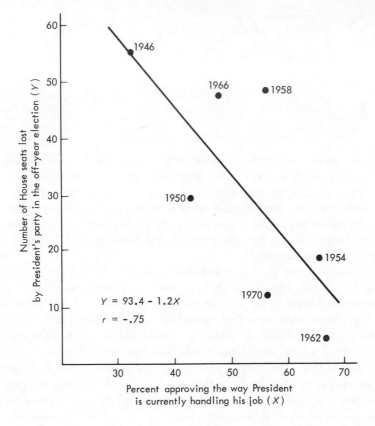

FIGURE **3-5**   President's approval rating vs. his party's seat loss

the details of the data. Note that the political party of the President lost seats in each of the seven midterm elections from 1946 to 1970. Sometimes the loss was small—in 1962, for example, the Democrats lost only four seats in the House of Representatives compared to what they had in 1960. In other elections, many seats were lost: the Democrats suffered a decline of 55 Congressional seats in 1946. The Republicans, under President Eisenhower, had a bad year in the 1958 midterm elections, losing 48 seats.

Is, then, the extent of the loss of congressional seats by the President's

TABLE 3-1
Congressional Seats and Presidential Popularity

Year	Seats held in House of Representatives by		Seats lost in midterm election by President's party
	Democrats	*Republicans*	
1944	243	190	
1946	188	246	Democrats lost 55
1948	263	171	
1950	234	199	Democrats lost 29
1952	213	221	
1954	232	203	Republicans lost 18
1956	234	201	
1958	283	153	Republicans lost 48
1960	262	175	
1962	258	176	Democrats lost 4
1964	295	140	
1966	248	187	Democrats lost 47
1968	243	192	
1970	255	180	Republicans lost 12

Year		President's popularity rating early September in off-year elections (percent approve)[a]
1946	Truman	32%
1950	Truman	43%
1954	Eisenhower	65%
1958	Eisenhower	56%
1962	Kennedy	67%
1966	Johnson	48%
1970	Nixon	56%

SOURCE: *Gallup Political Index,* October 1970, No. 64, page 16.

[a] Percent approve + percent disapprove + percent no opinion = 100 percent. The question is worded as follows: "Do you approve or disapprove of the way Blank is handling his job as President?"

party related to the approval rating of the President?[2] The correlation between popularity and seat loss is, for the seven elections, −.75,

[2] Two papers dealing with the issues raised by these data are: Angus Campbell, "Voters and Elections: Past and Present," *Journal of Politics,* 26 (November 1964); 745–57, and John E. Mueller, "Presidential Popularity from Truman to Johnson," *American Political Science Review,* 64 (March 1970), 18–34. See also, for a more sophisticated discussion, Douglas A. Hibbs, Jr., "Problems of Statistical Estimation and Casual Inference in Dynamic, Time-Series Regression Models," in Herbert Costner, ed., *Sociological Methodology, 1973–1974* (San Francisco: Jossey-Bass, 1974), ch. 10.

indicating that the lower the President's popularity, the more seats his party loses in the off-year elections. This is, for most political research at least, a rather strong, impressive correlation—although note that the correlation coefficient doesn't tell us *how much* a decline in the approval rating is associated with a loss of *how many* seats. The regression coefficient does, however, provide some help with this. The equation of the least-squares line is

$$\text{seats lost} = 93.36 - 1.20 \text{ (percent approving President)}$$

Figure 3-5 shows this line. The slope is -1.20, indicating that a one percent decline in the percent approving the current president is associated with a loss of about 1.2 seats in the upcoming off-year election. That regression coefficient is statistically significant:

$$t = \frac{\text{estimate of regression coefficient}}{\text{standard error}} = \frac{-1.20}{.48} = -2.50,$$

which, for five degrees of freedom, $(n - 2 = 7 - 2 = 5)$ exceeds the one-tailed t-value at the .05 level (-2.02).

Furthermore, the President's approval rating explains a good deal of the statistical variation in the outcome of the election:

$$r = -.75, \qquad r^2 = .56.$$

Thus the regression statistically explains 56 percent of the variation in the shifts in congressional seats.

All in all, this is a fairly impressive regression—a good correlation, a substantively meaningful regression coefficient that is statistically significant, and more than half the variance explained. Since it is so good, perhaps we can use the model for predictive purposes: taking the pre-election approval rating for the President and plugging into the regression equation to come up with an estimate of the loss of seats in the congressional election. This is all very nice, except that the prediction will not be a very secure one. Let us evaluate the quality of predictions based on the fitted line.

One way to get an idea of the predictive properties of the model is to look at the estimate of the variability about the line, the residual variance:

$$S^2_{Y|X} = \frac{\Sigma (Y_i - \hat{Y}_i)^2}{N - 2}.$$

The numerator is simply the unexplained variation. Taking the square root puts this statistic into the units in which the response variable, Y, is measured:

$$S_{Y|X} = 13.3 \text{ seats},$$

which is a rather large standard error in terms of predicting seats—especially when we start to consider confidence intervals of $\pm$ two standard errors.

Or, to evaluate the predictive quality of the model, we might look directly at the residuals for year of the observed data. Table 3-2 shows the computations. Once again, we see pretty substantial errors in prediction from the observed data—and, of course, the model itself is estimated so as to minimize the sum of squares of these residuals.

In short, then, we have here the beginnings of a good explanatory model, but it still needs improvement if it is to be useful for predictive purposes. How might we build a better, more complete model? Consider a model that also takes into account the economic conditions—for which some voters might hold the President and his party responsible—prevailing at the time of the election:

$$\text{seats lost} = \beta_0 + \beta_1 \text{ (presidential} + \beta_2 \text{ (economic}$$
$$\text{popularity)} \qquad \text{conditions)}.$$

Just as in the two-variable case, this three-variable model is estimated by least squares. Such a multiple regression, as it is called, will be examined in Chapter 4.

TABLE 3-2
Residual Analysis

Year	Y_i = observed seat loss by President's party	X_i = Presidential approval rating	$\hat{Y}_i$ = predicted seat loss for a given X_i, $\hat{Y}_i$ = $93.4 - 1.20X_i$	Residual[a] = observed − predicted = $Y_i - \hat{Y}_i$
1946	55 seats	32%	$93.4 - 1.2(32) = 55$	$55 - 55 =$ 0 seats
1950	29 seats	43%	$93.4 - 1.2(43) = 42$	$29 - 42 =$ 13 seats
1954	18 seats	65%	$93.4 - 1.2(65) = 15$	$18 - 15 =$ 3 seats
1958	48 seats	56%	$93.4 - 1.2(56) = 26$	$48 - 26 =$ 22 seats
1962	4 seats	67%	$93.4 - 1.2(67) = 13$	$4 - 13 =$ −9 seats
1966	47 seats	48%	$93.4 - 1.2(48) = 36$	$47 - 36 =$ 11 seats
1970	12 seats	56%	$93.4 - 1.2(56) = 26$	$12 - 26 =$ −14 seats

[a] Note that if residual > 0, the President's party lost more seats than predicted; if residual < 0, the President's party lost less seats than predicted.

Example 2: Lung Cancer and Smoking

THE FITTED LINE

Figure 3-6 shows the relationship between the death rate from lung cancer in 1950 and the cigarette comsumption in eleven countries in 1930. Cigarette consumption is lagged twenty years behind the death rate on the assumption that the carcinogenic consequences of smoking require a considerable length of time to show up. The fitted regression line is

$$\begin{bmatrix} \text{lung cancer deaths} \\ \text{per million people} \\ \text{in 1950 } (Y) \end{bmatrix} = .23 \begin{bmatrix} \text{cigarettes consumed} \\ \text{in 1930 } (X) \end{bmatrix} + 66,$$

standard error of slope = .07 $r^2 = .54$

The regression indicates that when cigarette consumption in 1930 from one country to another is greater by, say, 500 cigarettes per year per person, the lung cancer rate apparently increased by about 115 deaths per million in 1950.

SCALING OF VARIABLES AND INTERPRETATION OF
REGRESSION COEFFICIENTS

Note that in order to make an accurate interpretation of the regression coefficients, we must keep track of the units of measurement of each variable. For example, if the lung cancer rate were expressed as deaths per 100,000 people (instead of per 1,000,000), then the regression coefficient would be reduced by a corresponding factor of ten down to .023. This coefficient, although it is numerically smaller, reflects only the change in the scaling of the death rate—and the coefficient has exactly the same substantive meaning and importance as the original coefficient of .23. This obvious point is worth keeping in mind because some research reports are not particularly clear in reporting the units of measurement associated with each regression coefficient—and the reader must dig out the units of measurement and the scaling of the variables from the footnotes.

ANOTHER FITTED LINE: A REGRESSION WITHOUT
THE UNITED STATES

A further look at the scatterplot shows the rather strong effect of one extreme point in shifting the fitted line. The line is pulled down

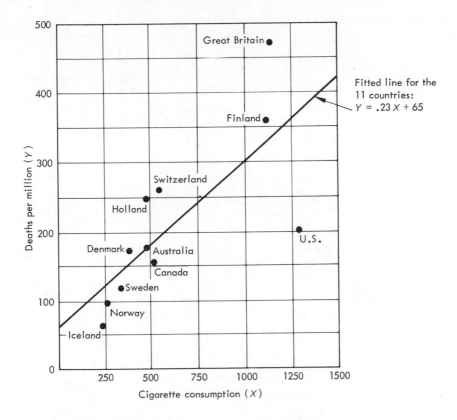

FIGURE 3-6 Crude male death rate for lung cancer in 1950 and per
capita consumption of cigarettes in 1930 in various
countries
SOURCE: R. Doll, "Etiology of Lung Cancer," *Advances in Cancer
Research*, 3 (1955), reprinted in *Smoking and Health*, Report of the
Advisory Committee to the Surgeon General (Washington: USGPO,
1964), p. 176.

by the low death rate for the United States. Removing that country
from the data and computing a new regression line based on the
remaining ten countries yields quite a different fitted line:

N = 10 Countries *(Without U.S.)*	*N = 11 Countries* *(With U.S.)*
$Y = .36 X + 14$	$Y = .23 X + 66$
$r^2 = .89$	$r^2 = .54$
Standard error of slope = .05	Standard error of slope = .07
Dotted line in Figure 3-7	Solid line in Figure 3-7

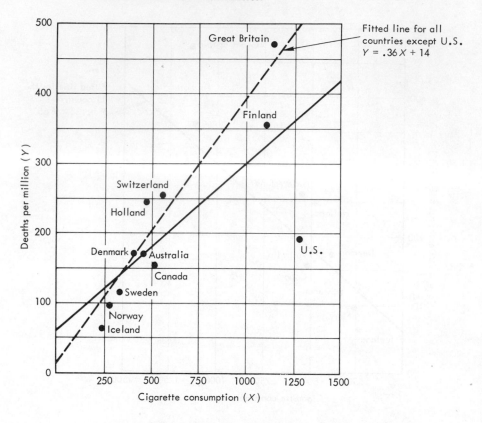

FIGURE 3-7   Lung cancer and cigarette consumption: fitted line for ten countries, omitting the United States

Note the great improvement in the explained variance in the regression based on the ten countries; a straight line really fits the ten quite well. Perhaps we should look more carefully into the conditions that make for a somewhat lower death rate than expected, given the amount of tobacco consumed, in the United States. That will be done below.

WHAT IF NOBODY SMOKED? INTERPRETING THE INTERCEPT

Let us return to consideration of the original regression for all eleven countries. Can we find out what the lung cancer rate might have been if there had been no smoking? Not very well with these particular data—for several reasons.

First, there is simply no experience at all with any countries consuming less tobacco per capita than Iceland, at 220 cigarettes per year per person in 1930. Obviously we want to be careful in

extending our results beyond the range of the data; some of the
particular problems of extrapolation are discussed in Chapter 2.

Second, one naive way to answer the question meets some difficulties
after a careful examination of the scatterplot. The naive approach
is to set cigarette smoking at zero in the fitted regression equation
and see what the lung cancer rate is. That rate is simply the intercept,
66 deaths per million per year. But note the pattern of countries
down at the low end with respect to smoking: the three lowest countries
have negative residuals, all lying below the fitted regression line.
Thus, in the countries with a low consumption of cigarettes, there
is some indication that a better-fitting curve would bend more sharply
downward; thus the straight line imposed on the data is a bit misleading
at the low end of the scale. This suggests that the rate would be
considerably lower than 66 if nobody smoked. Perhaps a better estimate
would be around 14 deaths per million—the intercept for the regression
line that excluded the United States. The exclusion of that outlying
value seems appropriate in estimating the intercept, since the outlier
is far from the region of interest and since the residuals near the
region of interest indicate that the extreme point has shifted the
regression line based on all the countries.

Note finally that the line is literally imposed on the data—and
just because we do the computations necessary to produce a slope
and an r^2, does not, of course, necessarily mean that the straight
line is the best curve to fit to the data or that the two variables
are, in fact, related in a linear fashion. In a later example, we will
use "linear" regression to fit some other curves to data.

What kind of data *would* satisfactorily estimate the death rate
from lung cancer if nobody smoked cigarettes? First, we need data
based on individuals—smokers and nonsmokers—to make comparisons of lung cancer rates. Second, it is important to make sure that
people susceptible—perhaps because of genetic or environmental
factors—to lung cancer are not also people who are more likely to
smoke. Thus we might compute the lung cancer rate for many different
sorts of people who are smokers or nonsmokers. Such differential
rates for different population groups could then be adjusted to the
population as a whole to estimate the lung cancer rate if, contrary
to fact, no one smoked.

ANALYZING THE RESIDUALS

Table 3-3 displays the original data, along with the predicted values
for the lung cancer rate (predicted on the basis of cigarette consumption) and the errors made in the prediction for each country. Note

TABLE 3-3
Residual Analysis

Country	Y_i = observed lung cancer deaths per million in 1950	X_i = cigarettes consumed per capita in 1930	$\hat{Y}_i$ = predicted lung cancer death rate for a given X_i, $\hat{Y}_i = .23X_i + 66$	Residual = observed − predicted = $Y_i - \hat{Y}_i$	
Iceland	58	220	.23(220) + 66 = 116	58 − 116 =	−58
Norway	90	250	.23(250) + 66 = 123	90 − 123 =	−33
Sweden	115	310	.23(310) + 66 = 137	115 − 137 =	−22
Canada	150	510	.23(510) + 66 = 183	150 − 183 =	−33
Denmark	165	380	.23(380) + 66 = 153	165 − 153 =	12
Australia	170	455	.23(455) + 66 = 170	170 − 170 =	0
United States	190	1280	.23(1280) + 66 = 359	190 − 359 =	−169
Holland	245	460	.23(460) + 66 = 171	245 − 171 =	74
Switzerland	250	530	.23(530) + 66 = 187	250 − 187 =	63
Finland	350	1115	.23(1115) + 66 = 321	350 − 321 =	29
Great Britain	465	1145	.23(1145) + 66 = 328	465 − 328 =	137

the large residuals for Great Britain and the United States and the negative residuals for the smaller values of tobacco consumption. The residuals add up to zero; the sum of the squared residuals is the smallest it can be—no other line can improve over the least-squares line in minimizing the sum of the squares of the residuals. These two properties of the residuals—

(1) $\Sigma (Y_i - \hat{Y}_i) = 0$, and
(2) $\Sigma (Y_i - \hat{Y}_i)^2$ is minimized

—are properties of all least-squares lines.

A further analysis of the residuals can be made by plotting the residuals against the predicted values ($\hat{Y}$) as shown in Figure 3-8. Sometimes such a display yields up more information because the reference line is a horizontal line rather than the tilted line fitted to the original scatterplot. Contemplation of the residuals reveals large errors in the prediction of the death rate for Great Britain and the United States. Great Britain had a much higher death rate than the United States in 1950, although the per capita consumption of cigarettes in the two countries in 1930 was roughly equal. What differences between the two countries might account for the differences in lung cancer death rates even though the tobacco consumption was roughly the same? A few possibilities include:

1. Differences in air pollution between the two countries.

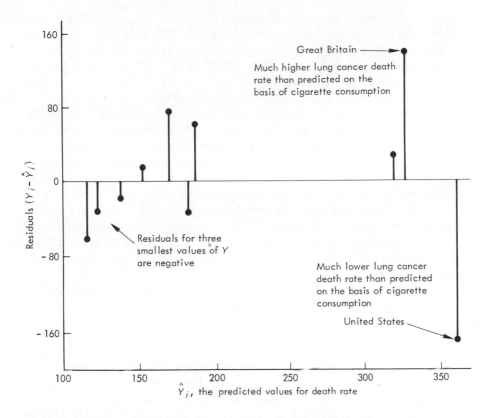

FIGURE **3-8**   Residuals vs. predicted values, lung cancer and smoking

2. Differences in the age distribution of the populations of the two countries. Since lung cancer occurs more frequently among older smokers, the rate of cancer might well be higher in a country that had a larger share of older people.

3. Differences in smoking habits (such as smoking cigarettes right down to the end) that expose the lungs to different doses of smoke from each cigarette consumed. Observers have reported that the British often smoke their cigarettes right down to the very end (probably because cigarettes are heavily taxed and very expensive in England) and also that the British tend to be "drooper" smokers—they let the cigarette droop from their mouth rather than placing it in an ashtray or holding in the hand. Some researchers compared the lengths of discarded cigarette butts in the two countries and discovered rather large differences in length, the American discards being considerably

longer (30.9 mm) than the British (18.7 mm).[3] Other studies found that "the mortality rate for lung cancer in England was especially high for the smokers who 'drooped' the cigarettes off the lip while they smoked, a habit which may result in the delivery of a greater dose of smoke from each cigarette."[4]

4. Differences in the composition of the tobacco.

5. Differences in the factors which mute or accentuate the health consequences of smoking. For example, construction workers and others exposed to the insulating material asbestos who also smoke have a very high risk of lung ailments—a much higher risk than expected by merely adding up the excess risk from smoking plus the excess risk from working with asbestos. (This extra risk coming from the *combination* of the two factors is called, in the statistical jargon, an "interaction effect.") Thus if more smokers in a country were exposed to asbestos, then that country would have a higher rate of lung cancer than expected on the basis of tobacco consumption alone.

6. Differences across countries in what medical symptoms doctors define or describe to be lung cancer.

VALUE OF THESE DATA AS EVIDENCE

These data have only a very modest value as evidence bearing on the relationship between smoking and lung cancer. Since the data are *aggregate, countrywide* figures, they provide very indirect evidence concerning the relationship between smoking and health among *individuals*. Furthermore, eleven data points aren't much to work with—and the exclusion of a single observation shifted the variance explained from 54 percent to 89 percent, indicating the sensitivity of the analysis to outlying observations.

A big worry about the sort of data presented in Figures 3-6 and 3-7 is *selection*—how were the eleven countries included in the analysis chosen from all the countries of the world? Why these eleven? Would the results be the same if more countries were selected? Or eleven different countries? With so few data points, the analysis is very fragile; just a couple of fresh observations divergent from the fitted line would cause the whole relationship to fall apart. Careful, if manipulative, selection of data points can easily generate pseudo-rela-

[3] Report of the Advisory Committee to the Surgeon General of the Public Health Service, *Smoking and Health* (Washington, D.C.: U.S. Government Printing Office, 1959), p. 177.

[4] *The Health Consequences of Smoking, 1969 Supplement to the 1967 Public Health Service Review* (Washington, D.C.: U.S. Government Printing Office), p. 57.

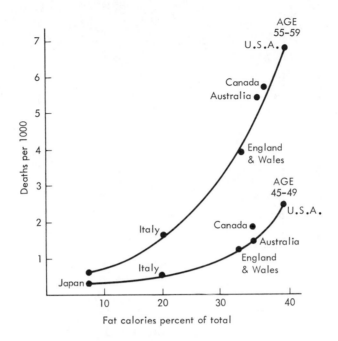

FIGURE 3-9   Mortality from degenerative heart disease (1948–1949,
men) in relation to fat calories consumed
SOURCES: Yerushalmy, *op. cit.* and Keys, *op. cit* (see p. 88).

tionships. Yerushalmy points out such an example:

Another important error often encountered in the literature is the
fallacy of utilizing evidence supporting a given hypothesis and
neglecting evidence contradicting it. An illustration is shown in Figure
[3-9]. In this case, the investigator selected six countries and correlated the percent of fat in the diet with the mortality of coronary
heart disease in these six countries. . . . On the face of it, the
correlation appears very striking, and indeed the author in reviewing
the data in Figure [3-9] makes the following strong statement: "The
analysis of international vital statistics shows a striking feature
when the national food consumption statistics are studied in parallel.
Then it appears that for men aged 40 to 60 or 70, that is, at the
ages when the fatal results of atherosclerosis are most prominent,
there is a remarkable relationship between the death rate from
degenerative heart disease and the proportion of fat calories in the
national diet. A regular progression exists from Japan through Italy,
Sweden, England and Wales, Canada, and Australia to the United
States. No other variable in the mode of life besides the fat calories
in the diet is known which shows anything like such a consistent
relationship to the mortality rate from coronary or degenerative heart
disease."

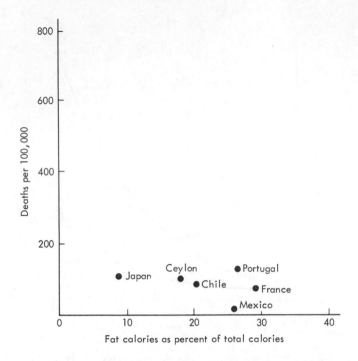

FIGURE 3-10   Six countries selected for equality in mortality from
                coronary heart disease, but differing greatly in con-
                sumption of fat calories in percent of total calories
SOURCE: Yerushalmy, *op cit.* (see p. 88).

The question arises how were these six countries selected. Further
investigation reveals that these six countries are not representative
of all countries for which the data are available. For example, it
is easy enough to select six other countries which differ greatly
in their dietary fat consumptions, but have nearly equal death rates
from coronary heart disease [Figure 3-10]. Similarly, six other
countries were easily selected which consumed nearly equal propor-
tions of dietary fat, but which differed widely in their death rates
from coronary heart disease [Figure 3-11]. This tendency of selecting
evidence biased for a favorable hypothesis is very common. For
example, investigations among the Bantu in Africa are often mentioned in support of the dietary fat hypothesis of coronary heart
disease, while observations on other African tribes, Eskimos, and
other groups which do not support the hypothesis are generally
ignored.

However, even when these errors are avoided and the studies are
well conducted, the conclusions which may be derived from observational studies have great limitations stemming primarily from non-
comparability of the self-formed groups. The phenomenon of self-
selection is the root of many of the difficulties. Were all other

complications eliminated, the inequalities between groups which result from self-selection would still leave in doubt inferences on causality. For example, in the study of the relationship of cigarette smoking to health, if we assume well-conducted investigations in which (a) large random samples of the population have been selected and the individuals correctly identified as smokers, nonsmokers, or past smokers, (b) the problem of nonresponse did not exist, (c) the population had been followed long enough to identify all cases of the disease in question, (d) no problems of misdiagnosis and misclassification existed, (e) and no one in the population had been lost from observation, then even under these ideal conditions, the inferences that may be drawn from the study are limited because the individuals being observed, rather than the investigator, made for themselves the crucial choice: smoker, nonsmoker, or past smoker.[5]

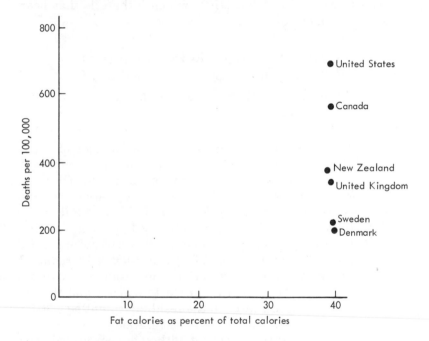

FIGURE 3-11 Six countries selected for equality in consumption of fat calories in percent of total calories, but differing greatly in mortality from coronary heart disease
SOURCE: Yerushalmy, *op. cit.* (see p. 88).

[5] J. Yerushalmy, "Self-Selection—A Major Problem in Observational Studies," in Lucien M. Lecam, Jerzy Neyman, and Elizabeth L. Scott, eds,. *Proceedings of the Sixth Berkeley Symposium on Mathematical Statistics and Probability, Biology and Health, Volume IV* (Berkeley and Los Angeles, California: University of California Press, 1972), pp. 332–33. The internal quotation is from A. Keys, "Atherosclerosis—A Problem in Newer Public Health," *Journal of Mt. Sinai Hospital,* 20 (1953), 134.

Still another reason for not taking our little analysis as serious evidence is that much better data are available to answer questions concerning the relationship between smoking and health. Smoking is probably the most carefully investigated public health problem there is; a vast amount of information has been gathered from health interviews with many people over many years, from autopsies, hospital records, animal studies, and so on. In other fields, where the amount and variety of evidence is less and the resources for collecting new data scarcer, the evidence of the sort examined here might represent the best available information and, furthermore, theories would have to stand or fall and decisions be made in the faint light of such analysis. Thus the overall importance of a particular piece of analysis varies in relation to what other evidence there is that bears on the question at hand.

Example 3: Increase in the Number of Radios and Increase in the Number of Mental Defectives, Great Britain, 1924–1937

The table shows a measure of the number of radios in the United Kingdom from 1924 to 1937 and the number of mental defectives per 10,000 people for the same years. These data form the basis for the discussion of "nonsense correlations" by the famous British statisticians, G. Udny Yule and M. G. Kendall.

The fit of the line is remarkably good, with a bit over 99% of the variation in number of mental defectives "explained" (in a statistical sense!) by the growth in the number of radios. Note the small, but systematic variation in the residuals, with the points weaving around the fitted line in clusters above and then below the fitted line. These "wrinkles" in the residuals might be worth pursuing if this were more than a nonsense correlation.

Why does this extremely strong, although nonsensical, relationship come about? This is a relationship formed by relating two increasing time series. In other words, the number of radios is increasing over time and also the number of mental defectives is increasing over time. Millions of other things are increasing over the time period from 1924 to 1937, including the population, the number of smokers, military expenditures in Europe, the number of patents issued, and the number of letters in the first name of the Presidents of the United States (Calvin, Herbert, and Franklin). For example, consider this regression:

Year	Number of radio receiver licenses issued (millions)	Number of notified mental defectives per 10,000 of estimated population
1924	1.350	8
1925	1.960	8
1926	2.270	9
1927	2.483	10
1928	2.730	11
1929	3.091	11
1930	3.647	12
1931	4.620	16
1932	5.497	18
1933	6.260	19
1934	7.012	20
1935	7.618	21
1936	8.131	22
1937	8.593	23

Figure 3-12 displays the regression line fitted to the above data:

$$\text{number of mental defectives per 10,000} = 2.20 \left[\text{number of radios (in millions)} \right] + 4.58,$$

$r^2 = .99,$ standard error of slope $= .08.$

$$\text{number of mental defectives per 10,000 in the United Kingdom, 1924–1937} = 5.90 \left(\begin{array}{c} \text{number of letters in the first name of the President of U.S., 1924–1937} \end{array} \right) - 26.44,$$

$r^2 = .89,$ standard error of slope $= .66.$

Yule and Kendall further observe:

. . . it might be argued that the period in question was one of great technical progress in many scientific fields; that one effect of this movement was the development of broadcasting and the general spread of the practice of listening evinced by the increased number of [radio] licenses taken out; that another effect was the greater interest in psychological ailments and increased facilities for treatment, resulting in either more discoveries of mental defect or greater readiness to submit cases to medical notice. Whether this is the right explanation is doubtful, but it is a possible rational explanation of what at first sight seems absurd.[6]

[6] G. Udny Yule and M. G. Kendall, *An Introduction to the Theory of Statistics* 14th ed., (London: Charles Griffin, 1950), p. 315–16.

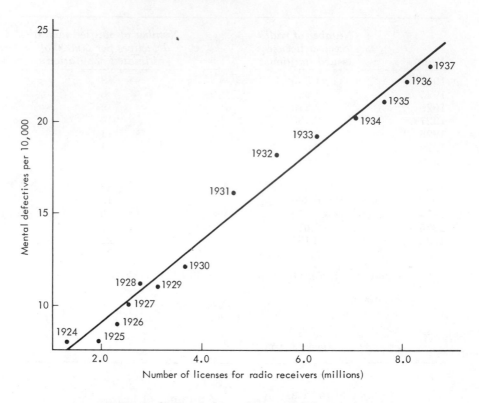

FIGURE 3-12   Radio receivers and mental defectives

Whether listening to the radio produced mental defectives (or, perhaps, whether the increase in number of mental defectives led to a greater demand for radios) is not answered by this regression of two increasing time series. And the relationship between the number of British mental defectives and the first names of American Presidents during 1924 to 1937 does not gain in credibility because the length of the name "explained" 87 percent of the variation in the number of mental defectives. What is clear, however, is that:

1. Even very high values of "explained" variance can occur without the slightest suspicion of a causal relationship between variables. There are times when a high value for r^2 might increase our degree of belief that there is a causal relationship, but this depends upon the substantive nature of the problem.
2. If nonsense goes into a statistical analysis, nonsense will come out. The nonsensical output will have all the statistical trappings, will look just as official, just as "scientific," and just as "objective" as a substantively useful regression. It is, however, the substance and not the form that is the important thing. As Justice Holmes

once wrote: "The only use of forms is to present their contents, just as the only use of a pint pot is to present the beer . . . and infinite meditation upon the pot will never give you the beer."

We have now seen regression techniques applied to several problems—automobile safety inspections, smoking and lung cancer, and radios and mental problems. These examples all served to illustrate certain aspects of the logic and mechanics of fitting a line to the relationship between two variables. It is now time to examine a more extensive regression analysis in action, going into detail on a serious problem. Such is our next application.

Example 4: The Relationship between Seats and Votes in Two-Party Systems[7]

Arrangements for translating votes into legislative seats almost always work to benefit the party winning the largest share of the votes. That the politically rich get richer has infuriated the partisans of minority parties, encouraged those favoring majority parliamentary rule, and, finally, bemused a variety of statisticians and political scientists who have tried to develop parsimonious descriptions and explanations of the inflation of the legislative power of the victorious party. Here we will use a linear regression model to describe how the votes of citizens are aggregated into legislative seats and also to estimate the bias in an electoral system.

Figure 3-13 shows the data used in the analysis.[8] These six scatterplots indicate that the relationship between seats and votes in most two-party systems displays four obvious characteristics:

1. As a party's share of the vote increases, its share of the seats also increases in a fairly regular fashion.

---

[7] A more extended version of this material appeared in Edward R. Tufte, "The Relationship Between Seats and Votes in Two-Party Systems," *American Political Science Review*, 68 (June 1973), 540–54.

[8] The election tabulations were collected from state and national yearbooks. The U.S. congressional returns have been collected together in Donald Stokes and Gudmund Iversen, "National Totals of Votes Cast for Democratic and Republican Candidates for the U.S. House of Representatives, 1866–1960," July 1962, mimeo, Survey Research Center, University of Michigan. *Congressional Directories* (Washington, D.C.: U.S. Government Printing Office) were used to update the Stokes-Iversen compilation and also as the source for tabulations requiring election returns in individual congressional districts. All percentages of the vote were computed from the votes received by the two major parties only.

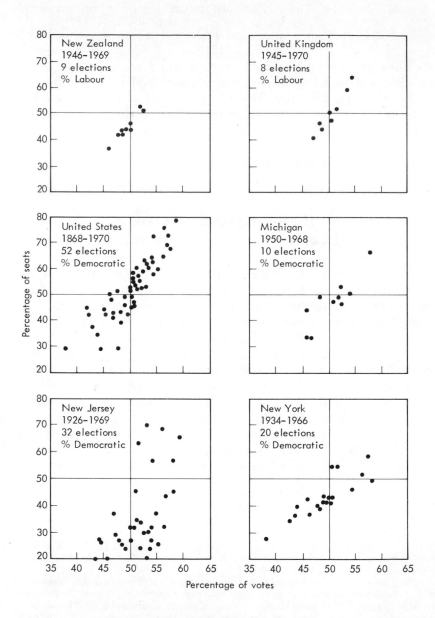

FIGURE 3-13 Seats and votes

2. The party that receives a majority of the votes usually receives a majority of parliamentary seats. Such was the case in 93 percent of the national elections and 53 percent of the state elections examined here. The points in the upper left and lower right quadrants represent those elections in which the party winning a majority of votes failed to take a majority of seats. New Jersey, like many other states prior to redistricting (and some after redistricting), shows many markedly biased outcomes, with the Democrats often winning fully three-fifths of the votes but less than one-third of the seats.

3. A party that wins a majority of votes generally wins an even larger majority of seats.

4. In most elections (100 percent in this series), the winning party receives less than 65 percent of the votes (although it may receive a much larger share of seats).

Even a casual inspection of the data displayed in Figure 3-13 indicates that almost any curve with a slope around two or three in the region from 35 to 65 percent of the vote for a party will fit the relationships rather well. Let us now examine the regression model.

The relationship between seats and votes is described most directly by a simple linear equation:

$$\begin{pmatrix} \text{percentage of seats for} \\ \text{a given political party} \end{pmatrix} = \beta_1 \begin{pmatrix} \text{percentage of votes} \\ \text{for that party} \end{pmatrix} + \beta_0 .$$

The estimate of the slope, $\hat{\beta}_1$, measures the percentage change in seats corresponding to a change of one percent in the votes for a party. Thus $\hat{\beta}_1$ estimates the *swing ratio* or the *responsiveness* of the partisan composition of parliamentary bodies to changes in the partisan division of the vote in two-party systems. For example, the swing ratio during the last twelve U.S. congressional elections is 1.9, indicating that a net shift of 1.0 percent in the national vote for a party has typically been associated with a net shift of 1.9 percent in congressional seats for a party.

In addition, the fitted line provides an estimate of another important parameter of the electoral system: the bias for or against a particular party in the translation of votes into seats. Setting the percentage of seats at 50 percent and solving for the percentage of votes in the equation of the fitted line tells one the share of the vote that a party typically needs in order to win a majority of seats in the legislative body. The difference between this number and 50 percent is the *bias* or *party advantage*, as illustrated in Figure 3-14. For

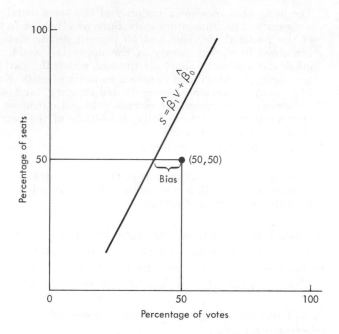

FIGURE 3-14   The fitted seats-votes line

example, in recent congressional elections, the Democrats have typically needed only about 48 percent of the national vote in order to
win a majority of House seats; thus the bias or party advantage
is about 2 percent. Later we will explain some of the variations in
the swing ratio and bias for different electoral systems over the years.

Note that we are using the estimate of the slope in the linear
model in order to estimate the swing ratio; the analogue of the intercept
in the linear model is, in this case, the bias. Thus both the parameters
estimated by the linear regression model are useful in this analysis.

One minor defect of the linear fit is that in general the fitted
line will not pass through the end points (0 percent votes, 0 percent
seats) and (100 percent votes, 100 percent seats), which are on the
seats-votes curve by definition. Although slightly inelegant, this
shortcoming is hardly troublesome—especially since parties in two-
party systems almost never get less than 35 percent of the vote nor
more than 65 percent of it.[9] The clear advantage of the linear fit

[9] A "logit" model dealing with this problem is described in Example 6 of
this chapter.

is that it yields two politically meaningful numbers, the swing ratio and the bias, that can be compared over time and electoral systems.

Table 3-4 records the fitted lines for a variety of elections. The swing ratios and the biases show considerable variation both between electoral systems and within some systems over time. Among the countries, Great Britain has the greatest swing ratio at 2.8. In the United States the swing ratio has been about two, although, as we shall see later, there is evidence that in the last few elections the swing ratio has decreased considerably. The U.K. electoral system shows little bias; in the United States a persistent bias has favored

TABLE 3-4

Linear Fit for the Relationship between Seats and Votes

	$\hat{\beta}_1$ Swing ratio and (standard error)	r^2	Percentage votes required to give the indicated party a majority of seats in the legislature	Advantaged party and amount of advantage
Great Britain, 1945–1970	2.83 (.29)	.94	50.2% Labour	Conservatives, .2%
New Zealand, 1946–1969	2.27 (.27)	.91	51.4% Labour	National, 1.4%
United States, 1868–1970	2.39 (.21)	.71	49.1% Democrats	Democrats, 0.9%
United States, 1900–1970	2.09 (.14)	.87	48.0% Democrats	Democrats, 2.0%
United States, 1948–1970	1.93 (.29)	.81	48.8% Democrats	Democrats, 1.2%
Michigan, 1950–1968	2.06 (.41)	.76	52.1% Democrats	Republicans, 2.1%
New Jersey, 1926–1947	2.10 (.44)	.53	61.3% Democrats	Republicans, 11.3%
New Jersey, 1947–1969	3.65 (.89)	.63	52.0% Democrats	Republicans, 2.0%
New York, 1934–1966	1.28 (.19)	.73	54.3% Democrats	Republicans, 4.3%

the Democratic party—partially the result of that party's victories in small congressional districts and in districts with low turnouts. In Michigan, New Jersey, and New York there have been large biases favoring the Republicans and a great deal of variation in swing ratios. The relationship between votes and seats is weaker for the three states than for the three countries; in fact, in the states during some time periods there was virtually no correlation between the share of seats that a party won in the legislature and the share of votes it had received at the polls! In more recent elections, however, there was a fairly strong relationship between seats and votes in all three states—probably the result of new rules and practices for districting.

THE SWING RATIO IN RECENT CONGRESSIONAL ELECTIONS

We now examine changes in the swing ratio in elections for the U.S. House of Representatives. Table 3-5 shows estimates of swing ratio and bias for congressional elections for the last hundred years. It appears that a shift—in fact, a rather striking shift—in the relationship between seats and votes has taken place in the last decade. The 1966–1970 triplet displays the second lowest swing ratio of the 17 election triplets since 1870. No doubt the recent elections provide a somewhat narrow range of electoral experience; the Democrats won with votes between 50.9 and 54.3 percent (a range in votes that is the fifth smallest of the 17 triplets). Until the Republicans control Congress or the Democrats win more decisively, the "new" swing ratio and bias will not be well estimated. The bias is a spectacular 7.9 percent, reflecting the two close votes that yielded the Democrats a substantial party majority in the House. The estimate of the bias for the 1966–1970 election triplet is, however, somewhat more insecure than for previous blocs of elections because the error of the estimated bias is proportional to the reciprocal of the swing ratio—and in this case the swing ratio is moderately small.

Compared with all the other performances of the electoral systems examined here, a system with a swing ratio of .7 and a bias of 7.9 percent describes a set of electoral arrangements that is both quite unresponsive to shifts in the preferences of voters (as expressed in their party votes for their representatives) and, at the same time, badly biased. How did the low value of the swing ratio for 1966–1970 come about? Certainly the Democratic party, after their substantial gain in votes (3.4 percent) and relatively tiny gain—given the "normal" swing ratio exceeding 2.0—in seats (3.2 percent) would like to know what happened in 1970. And for Republicans, 1966 and 1968 need

TABLE 3-5
Three Elections at a Time: Estimates of Swing Ratio and Bias

Years of elections	Swing ratio	Percentage of votes to elect 50% seats for Democrats	Size of Democratic party advantage
1870–74	6.01	51.4%	−1.4%
1876–80	1.48	50.0%	.0%
1882–86	3.30	50.8%	−.8%
1888–92	6.01	50.9%	−.9%
1894–98	2.82	51.7%	−1.7%
1900–04	2.23	50.1%	−.1%
1906–10	4.21	48.8%	1.2%
1912–16	2.39	48.8%	1.2%
1918–22	1.96	47.6%	2.4%
1924–28 [a]	−5.75 [a]	40.8% [a]	9.2% [a]
1930–34	2.28	45.9%	4.1%
1936–40	2.50	47.1%	2.9%
1942–46	1.90	48.1%	1.9%
1948–52	2.82	49.5%	.5%
1954–58	2.35	50.1%	−.1%
1960–64	1.65	47.4%	2.6%
1966–70	.71	42.1%	7.9%

[a] The figures estimated for the 1924–1928 election triplet are peculiar because of the extremely narrow range of variation in the share of the vote (42.1, 41.6, and 42.8 percent) during that period. The average range within an election triplet is about 6 percent.

explanation: after all, they managed to make the national division of the vote very close but in neither year were they able to win even 45 percent of the House seats.

The swing ratio indicates the potential for turnover in representation. The smaller the swing ratio, the less responsive the party distribution of seats is to shifts in the preferences of voters. The extreme case is a swing ratio near zero; such a flat seats-votes curve means that the distribution of seats does not change with the distribution of votes. Figure 3-15 shows the strong relationship between the swing ratio and the turnover in the House of Representatives for election triplets since 1870. Note the steady drift downward over the years in both the swing ratio and the turnover. Since 1948, the swing ratio has shifted from 2.8 to 2.4 to 1.7, and, most recently, to 0.7. Similarly the turnover in the House has declined, reflecting the long-run decrease in the intensity of competition for congressional seats.[10]

One element in the job security of incumbents is their ability to exert significant control over the drawing of district boundaries; indeed, some recent redistricting laws have been described as the Incumbent Survival Acts of 1974. It is hardly surprising that legislators, like businessmen, collaborate with their nominal adversaries to eliminate

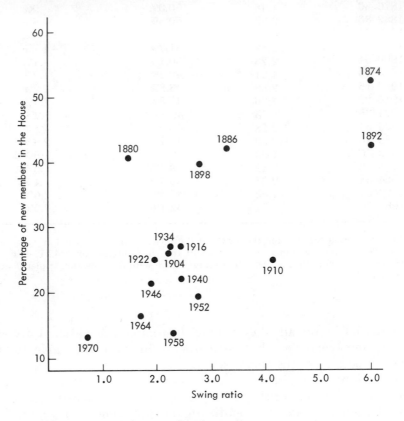

FIGURE 3-15   Turnover and swing ratio

dangerous competition. Ironically, reapportionment rulings have given incumbents new opportunities to construct secure districts for them-

[10] See: Stokes; Nelson W. Polsby, "The Institutionalization of the U.S. House of Representatives," *American Political Science Review*, 62 (March 1968), 144–68; and David R. Mayhew, "Congressional Representation: Theory and Practice in Drawing the Districts," in *Reapportionment in the 1970s*, ed. N. Polsby, pp. 249–90.

selves, leading to a reduction in turnover that is, in turn, reflected in the sharply reduced swing ratio of the last few elections. One apparent consequence is the remarkable change in the shape of the distribution of congressional votes in recent elections. Prior to 1964, the congressional vote by district was distributed the way everyone expects votes to be distributed: a big clump of relatively competitive districts in the middle, tailing off away from 50 percent with some peaks at the ends of the distribution for districts without an opposition candidate:

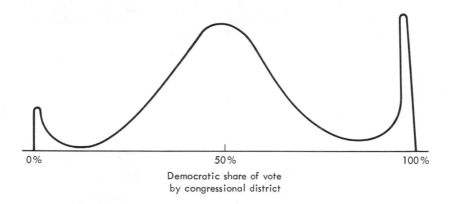

Democratic share of vote
by congressional district

In recent elections the shape of the distribution of the vote by district has changed; Figure 3-16 shows the movement of district outcomes away from the danger area of 50 percent in recent years— note the development of bimodality in the 1968 and 1970 district vote compared to previous years (the left peak contains the Republican safe seats; the right peak contains the Democratic safe seats). Perhaps the best way to see how this pattern developed over time is to array the vote distributions over the years and riffle through them—like an old-time peep show—and watch the middle of the distribution sag and the areas of incumbent safety bulge in the more recent elections.

Many states, in part through recent reapportionments, have practically eliminated political competition for congressional seats—even compared to the relatively small proportion of competitive seats in the past. In the 1970 elections in Michigan, for example, not one of the 19 districts was a close contest; the *most* marginal Republican victor won 56 percent of the vote and the *most* marginal Democrat won fully 70% of the vote in his district. In Illinois, the most closely

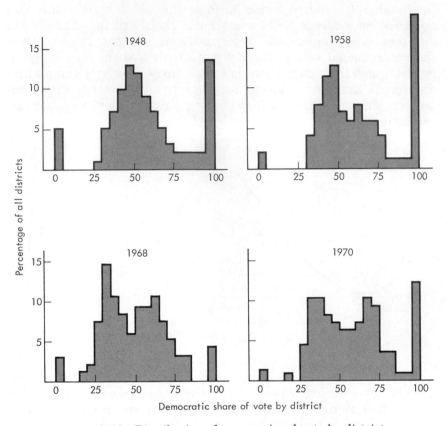

FIGURE 3-16   Distribution of congressional vote by district

contested race in all 24 congressional districts in 1970 was a 54–46 division of the vote; in contrast, in 1960, seven districts had closer races than that. The closest 1970 race in Pennsylvania was 55–45; in Ohio, 53–47.

In conclusion, then, we have seen here how the linear regression model can be used to measure two important qualities of an electoral system—the responsiveness and the partisan bias of the system. These two measurements might even be used by the courts to evaluate the fairness and the effectiveness of redistricting plans submitted to the courts.

This example has shown the economy of the regression model, in which the estimate of the slope takes us quickly to the central political issues in the data. There was little to learn from a correlation coefficient in this case (and in many others), for we already knew that there was a strong relationship between how many votes and how many seats a party received. In contrast to the correlation coefficient, the regression model gave us a measure permitting politically meaningful comparisons across different political systems. Note also that a correlational analysis misses the method of assessing the partisan bias—an estimate which flows naturally from the regression model. Finally, look back at those four histograms in Figure 3-16. Note how informative they are with respect to the performance of the electoral system and how directly they make the point. Such is generally the case. Pictures of the data—charts, scatterplots, histograms, or just the values of a variable marked out on a line—are powerful aids to analysis. They also are easy to produce, either by hand or by computer.

Example 5: Comparing the Slope and the Correlation Coefficient

Both the correlation coefficient, r, and the slope of the fitted line, β_1, are numerical summaries of the relationship between two variables. The slope, since it expresses the relationship in terms of the units in which X and Y are measured, is often a more useful summary measure than the correlation. This was true in the examples dealing with midterm congressional elections and the translation of votes into seats. In those examples the slope carried the important message in the data. Such interpretations of the slope require, however, that the units of measurement of the X and Y variables make some sort of interpretative sense.

For example, in examining responses to an interview questionnaire—and correlating relationships over the different responses to questions—it is difficult to interpret a measure of the rate of change on the intensity of feeling on one question with respect to the intensity of feeling on another. In such a case, the correlation coefficient may be more appropriate.

John Tukey has expressed these views strongly:

> . . . [M]ost correlation coefficients should never be calculated. . . . [C]orrelation coefficients are justified in two and only two circumstances, when they are regression coefficients, or when measurement of one or both variables on a determinate scale is hopeless. . . . The other area in which correlation coefficients are prominent

includes psychometrics and educational testing in general. This is surely a situation where determinate scales are hopeless.[11]

The correlation coefficient, r, can be interpreted in a number of ways. Its square, r^2, is the proportion of variance in the response variable explained by the describing variable. Or it can be viewed as the average covariation of standardized variables:

$$r = \frac{1}{N} \sum_{i=1}^{N} \left(\frac{X_i - \bar{X}}{S_X} \right) \left(\frac{Y_i - \bar{Y}}{S_Y} \right).$$

That is, each observation is rescaled and measured in terms of how many standard deviations it is from the mean—for a given observation (X_i, Y_i):

$$\frac{X_i - \bar{X}}{S_X} \quad \text{and} \quad \frac{Y_i - \bar{Y}}{S_Y}.$$

The product of the rescaled variables is averaged over all observations to yield the correlation coefficient.

Both the correlation coefficient and the slope can be dominated by a few extreme values in the data. Since we are working with products of deviations from the mean, a data point far from the mean on both variables can virtually determine the value of r and β_1. Thus sometimes r and β_1 do not provide very good summaries of the relationship between X and Y. They fail when the relationship is nonlinear and when the data contain extreme outlying values.[12] The problems are easily detected from a scatterplot of the data. Thus one practical moral is that every calculation of r and β_1 should also involve an inspection of the scatterplot.

Let us now look at a series of scatterplots. First are examples in which the data are well described by the linear model: the data are

[11] J. W. Tukey, "Causation, Regression, and Path Analysis," in O. Kempthorne, et al., eds., *Statistics and Mathematics in Biology* (Ames, Iowa: Iowa State College Press, 1956), pp. 38–39.

[12] In the case of many nonlinear scatterplots, the data can be transformed and the linear model estimated. Outliers can be treated by transformations, by removing them from the analysis, or by "Windsorizing" them (setting the most extreme value on a variable to the next most extreme). See Joseph B. Kruskal, "Special Problems of Statistical Analysis: Transformations of Data," *International Encyclopedia of the Social Sciences* (New York: Macmillan, 1968), vol. 15, 182–93; and F. J. Anscombe, "Outliers," *ibid.*, 178–82.

roughly oriented around a straight line with no extreme outliers (Figure 3-17).

We finally turn to some data sets for which the correlation and the fitted line fail to summarize the data effectively. Figure 3-18 shows three scatterplots with widely divergent patterns of relationship between X and Y. the first plot shows no relationship, discounting the one extreme outlier on both measures. The second plot suggests a moderately strong linear relationship between X and Y. The third plot reveals a rather marked curvilinear relationship between X and Y, revealing that as X increases, Y gets bigger even faster. Despite the great variation in the visual message, *the correlation between X and Y* is the same in all three cases. Also, the slopes do not differ greatly in the three cases.

Often a set of data for which the linear model is not immediately applicable can be transformed so the linear model is valuable. Or, to put it the other way around: many models with nonlinearities in the variables can be estimated by so-called "linear" regression.

ᵀor example, suppose we work with the logarithm of the one of the variables and have the model

$$Y = \beta_0 + \beta_1 \log X.$$

This model is estimated by letting $X' = \log X$ and then performing the usual least-squares regression for the model

$$Y = \beta_0 + \beta_1 X'.$$

Thus the criticism sometimes made that linear regression "assumes linearity" is a bit misleading, since the assumption can, in fact, be checked—and, if false, the model then redesigned for purposes of estimation. In fact, a better name for what this chapter has been all about is "fitting curves to relationships between two variables."

In summary, then, fitting lines to relationships between variables is often a useful and powerful method of summarizing a set of data. Regression analysis fits naturally with the development of causal explanations, simply because the research worker must, at a minimum know, what he or she is seeking to explain. The regression model is surprisingly flexible and we now illustrate methods that increase its range of application.

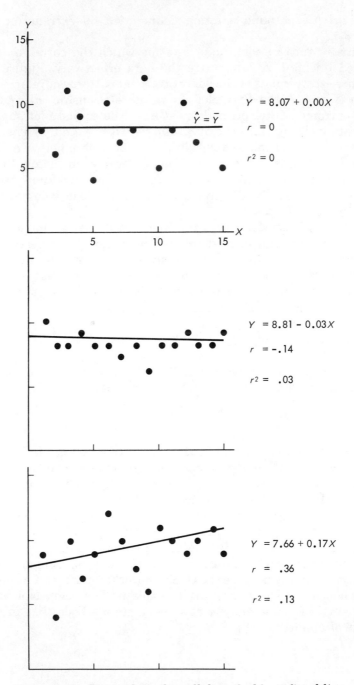

FIGURE 3-17   Data relatively well described by a fitted line

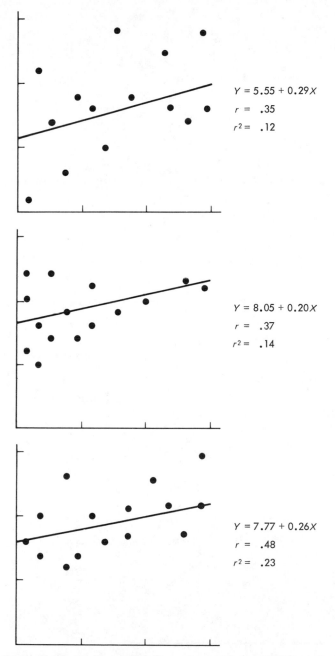

$Y = 5.55 + 0.29X$
$r = .35$
$r^2 = .12$

$Y = 8.05 + 0.20X$
$r = .37$
$r^2 = .14$

$Y = 7.77 + 0.26X$
$r = .48$
$r^2 = .23$

FIGURE 3–17   Data relatively well described by a fitted line

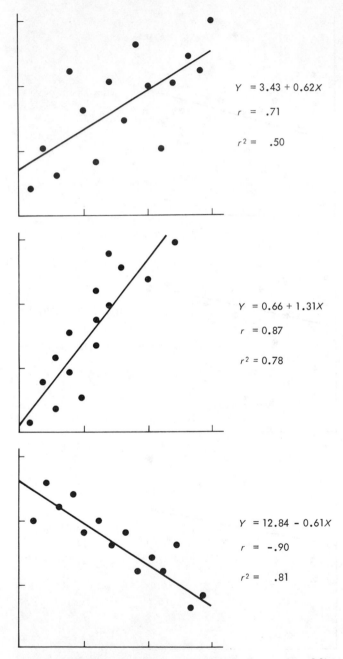

$Y = 3.43 + 0.62X$

$r = .71$

$r^2 = .50$

$Y = 0.66 + 1.31X$

$r = 0.87$

$r^2 = 0.78$

$Y = 12.84 - 0.61X$

$r = -.90$

$r^2 = .81$

FIGURE 3-17   Data relatively well described by a fitted line

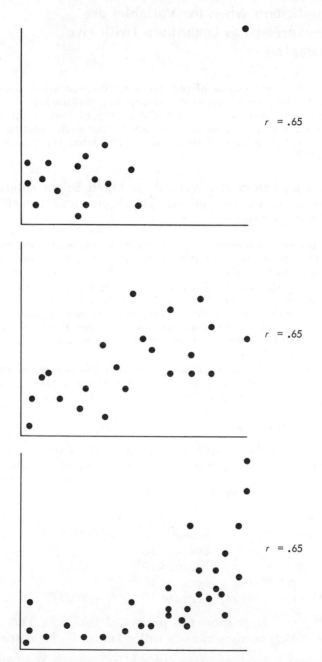

FIGURE 3-18   Three scatterplots with the same correlation

Example 6: Interpretation of Regression Coefficients when the Variables are Re-expressed as Logarithms (with Five Examples)

> Data that are *counts* of populations, vital statistics, census data, and the like are almost always improved by taking logs. . . . Charles Winsor frequently prescribed the taking of logs of all naturally occurring counts (plus *one*, to handle that embarrassing quantity *zero*) before analyzing them—no matter what the sources [of the data].[13]

Often the logarithm of a variable is taken before entering that variable in a regression analysis. The logarithmic transformation serves several purposes:

1. The resulting regression coefficients sometimes have a more useful theoretical interpretation compared to a regression based on unlogged variables.
2. Badly skewed distributions—in which many of the observations are clustered together combined with a few outlying values on the scale of measurement—are transformed by taking the logarithm of the measurements so that the clustered values are spread out and the large values pulled in more toward the middle of the distribution.
3. Some of the assumptions underlying the regression model and the associated significance tests are better met when the logarithm of the measured variables is taken.

REMEMBERING LOGARITHMS

The logarithm to the base b of a number x, written as $\log_b x$, is the power to which the base must be raised to yield x. Thus

$\log_{10} 1000 = 3$, because $10^3 = 1000$.

Similarly:

$\log_{10} 10,000 = 4$,   because $10^4 = 10,000$.
$\log_{10} 1 = 0$,   because $10^0 = 1$.
$\log_{10} 2 = .30103$,   because $10^{.30103} = 2$.
$\log_{10} 2000 = 3.30103$,   because $10^{3.30103} = 200$.
$\log_{10} 20,000 = 4.30103$, because $10^{4.30103} = 20,000$.

In short, then, logarithms are powers of the base. The base 10, the base e (which forms what are called "natural" logarithms), and

[13]Forman S. Acton, *Analysis of Straight-Line Data* (New York: Wiley, 1959), p. 223.

the base 2 are the ones most commonly used. Logs to the base 2 take the following form:

$\log_2 8 = 3$,   because $2^3 = 8$.

The logarithm of zero does not exist (regardless of the base) and therefore must be avoided. In logging variables with some zero values (especially those deriving from counts), the most common procedure is to add one to all the observations of the variable.

Finally, we should recall the following rules for manipulation of logarithms:

For $x > 0$ and $y > 0$:

$$\log xy = \log x + \log y.$$

For example,

$$\begin{aligned} \log 20{,}000 &= \log (2)(10{,}000) \\ &= \log 2 + \log 10{,}000 \\ &= .30103 + 4 \\ &= 4.30103. \end{aligned}$$

$$\log \frac{x}{y} = \log x - \log y.$$

$$\log x^n = n \log x.$$

Let us first look at the effect of taking logarithms on the measurement scale of a single variable. Figure 3-19 shows the relationship between X and $\log X$; and Table 3-6 (page 111) tabulates the populations of some 29 countries of the world along with the logarithm of population. Note how the logarithmic transformation pulls the extremely large values in toward the middle of the scale and spreads the smaller values out in comparison to the original, unlogged values of the variable. Although the transformation preserves the rank ordering of the countries with respect to population, it still does produce quite a major change in the scaling of the variable here: the correlation between the population and the logarithm of population for the 29 countries is .68.

One reason for expressing population size here as a power of ten (that is, logging size to the base ten) is simply for convenience: if our scatterplots are going to include and differentiate between Iceland and Norway as well as the United States and India, then something must be done to compress the extreme end of the distribution. Logging

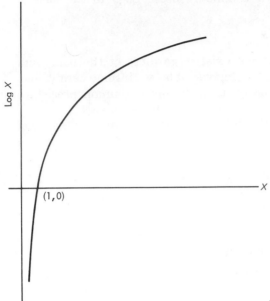

FIGURE 3-19 X vs. log X

size transforms the original skewed distribution into a more symmetrical one by pulling in the long right tail of the distribution toward the mean. The short left tail is, in addition, stretched. The shift toward symmetrical distribution produced by the log transform is not, of course, merely for convenience. Symmetrical distributions, especially those that resemble the normal distribution, fulfill statistical assumptions that form the basis of statistical significance testing in the regression model. Figure 3-20 shows the contrast between the logged and unlogged frequency distributions of population.

Logging skewed variables also helps to reveal the patterns in the data. Figure 3-21 shows the relationship between the population size of a country and the size of its parliament—for the unlogged and the logged variables. Note how the rescaling of the variables by taking logarithms reduces the nonlinearity in the relationship and removes much of the clutter resulting from the skewed distributions on both variables; in short, the transformation helps clarify the relationship between the two variables. It also, as we will see now, leads to a theoretically meaningful regression coefficient.

Much of the value of the logarithmic transformation derives from its contribution to the testing of theoretical models by means of linear

TABLE 3-6
Population, 29 Countries, 1970

Country	Population	Log (Population)
Iceland	200,000	5.30
Luxembourg	400,000	5.60
Trinidad and Tobago	1,100,000	6.04
Costa Rica	1,800,000	6.25
Jamaica	2,000,000	6.30
New Zealand	2,800,000	6.45
Lebanon	2,800,000	6.45
Israel	2,900,000	6.46
Uruguay	2,900,000	6.46
Ireland	3,000,000	6.48
Norway	3,900,000	6.59
Finland	4,700,000	6.67
Denmark	4,900,000	6.69
Switzerland	6,300,000	6.80
Austria	7,400,000	6.87
Sweden	8,000,000	6.90
Belgium	9,700,000	6.99
Chile	9,800,000	6.99
Australia	12,500,000	7.10
Netherlands	13,000,000	7.11
Canada	21,400,000	7.33
Philippines	38,100,000	7.58
France	51,100,000	7.71
Italy	53,700,000	7.73
United Kingdom	56,000,000	7.75
West Germany	58,500,000	7.77
Japan	103,500,000	8.02
United States	204,600,000	8.31
India	554,600,000	8.74

regression.[14] In interpreting regression coefficients of such models when the variables are logged, we have the following possibilities:

		Describing variable (X)	
		Logged	Not logged
Response variable (Y)	Logged	I	II
	Not logged	III	IV

[14] For further information see J. Johnston, *Econometric Methods*, 2d ed. (New York: McGraw-Hill, 1972), chap. 3; N. R. Draper and H. Smith, *Applied Regression*

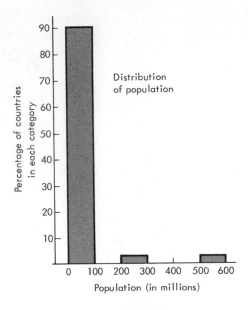

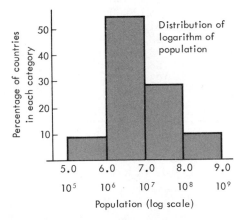

FIGURE 3-20   Logged vs. unlogged frequency distributions

Analysis (New York: Wiley, 1966); J. W. Richards, *Interpretation of Technical Data* (New York: Van Nostrand-Reinhold, 1967); and Joseph B. Kruskal, *op. cit.* For applications to political data see Hayward Alker and Bruce Russett, "Multifactor Explanations of Social Change," in Russett et. al., *World Handbook of Political and Social Indicators* (New Haven, Conn.: Yale, 1964), 311–21.

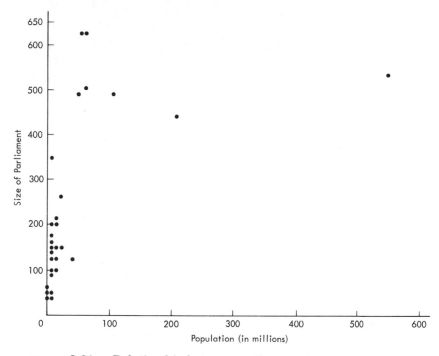

Figure **3-21a**   Relationship between parliamentary size and population, 29 democracies—neither variable logged

Case IV is simply the usual two-variable regression model with both variables unlogged. We now consider the three cases in which at least one of the variables in the analysis is logged.

CASE I—BOTH THE DESCRIBING AND THE RESPONSE
VARIABLES LOGGED

In the model

$$\log Y = \beta_1 \log X + \beta_0,$$

we estimate β_1 and β_0 by ordinary least squares by letting $X' = \log X$ and $Y' = \log Y$, which yields the linear form

$$Y' = \beta_1 X' + \beta_0.$$

How is the regression coefficient in the double-log case interpreted? Beginning with the regression

$$\log_{10} Y = \beta_1 \log_{10} X + \beta_0$$

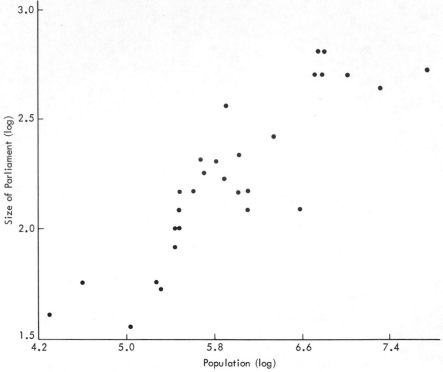

Figure **3-21b**   Relationship between parliamentary size (log) and population (log)—both variables logged.

and taking derivatives,

$$\frac{dY}{dX}\frac{1}{Y}\log_e 10 = \beta_1(\log_e 10)\frac{1}{X} + 0,$$

yields $\dfrac{dY}{dX}\dfrac{X}{Y} = \beta_1$

or $\beta_1 = \dfrac{dY/Y}{dX/X}$, which is the *elasticity* of Y with respect to X.

Thus β_1 measures the *percentage* change in Y with respect to a *percentage* change in X. The slope can be written approximately as

$$\beta_1 = \frac{\Delta Y/Y}{\Delta X/X}$$

and, when both the describing and the response variables are logged, the estimate of the slope assesses the proportionate change in Y resulting from a proportionate change in X. Note how this differs from the usual interpretation of the slope when both variables are unlogged (case IV):

$$\beta_1 = \frac{\Delta Y}{\Delta X}.$$

It is important to realize that fitting the model

$$\log Y = \beta_1 \log X + \beta_0,$$

does not *test* the assumption that there is, in fact, a proportionate relationship between X and Y. The logic is: *Assuming that there is a proportionate relationship between X and Y,* what is the best estimate of that proportionality or elasticity? Thus the regression answers the quantitative question by estimating a parameter in a model—on the assumption that the model is correct. We choose between competing models by comparing their goodness of fit, by thinking about their theoretical underpinnings, and by adding sufficient degrees of freedom in the model to allow the data to indicate the best fit. Our first example illustrates this point.

EXAMPLE 1 FOR THE LOG-LOG CASE: RELATIONSHIP BETWEEN PARLIAMENTARY SIZE AND POPULATION SIZE

Figure 3-22 shows the relationship, with both variables logged, between the population of a country and the size of its parliament for 135 countries of the world.[15] This relationship appears nearly linear in logarithms, and the fitted line is

$$\log_{10} \text{members} = .396 \log_{10} \text{population} - .564,$$

which explains, statistically at least, some 70.7 percent of the variation

---

[15] A discussion of the substantive issues involved in this relationship is found in Robert A. Dahl and Edward R. Tufte, *Size and Democracy* (Stanford, Calif.: Stanford University Press, 1973), Ch. 7.

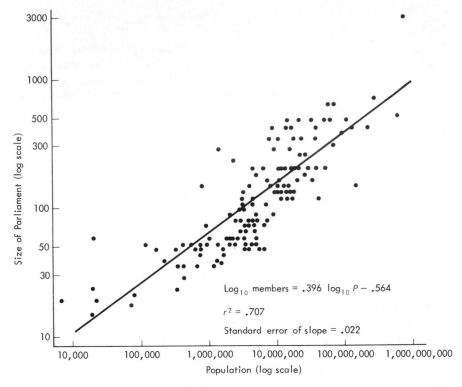

$$\text{Log}_{10} \text{ members} = .396 \text{ log}_{10} P - .564$$

$$r^2 = .707$$

Standard error of slope = .022

FIGURE 3-22   Population vs. parliament size—both variables logged

in parliamentary size. The estimated slope, .396, indicates that if a country was one percent above the average population of all countries, it was also typically about .4 percent above average with respect to size of parliament. A slightly more daring interpretation is to say that a change of one percent in population typically produces a change of .4 percent in parliamentary size.

Figure 3-22 and the residuals from the fitted line show a bend in the data—there is something of a threshold in the size of parliament for the smaller countries. For most of the countries with less than one million people, the observed points lie above the fitted line, indicating a tendency toward a minimum size of parliament around thirty members. We can improve upon the first fitted line for the 135 countries by examining some models that avoid the assumption of constant elasticity for all values of population (P) and take the bend in the data into account. One good approach, upon observing

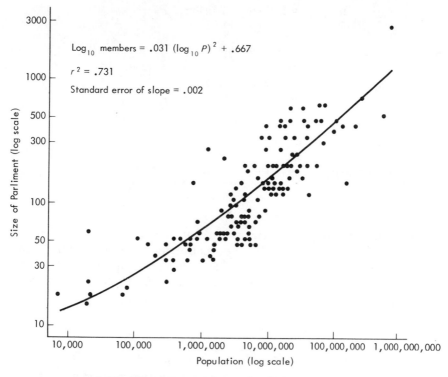

FIGURE **3-23**   Fitted line with quadratic term

a curve in the data, is to introduce a quadratic term. The following fit, with its $(\log P)^2$ term, is our second model:

$$\log M = .031(\log P)^2 + .667.$$

Figure 3-23 shows the fit. This regression predicts 73.1 percent of the variation in the logarithm of parliamentary size—an improvement of 2.4 percentage points over the first model with no increase in the number of coefficients used in the model. What is the interpretation of this result? In particular, what does the regression coefficient mean? We get the answer by applying the same logic used in deriving the elasticity in the log-log case. The model is

$$\log_{10} M = \beta_0 + \beta_1 (\log_{10} P)^2.$$

Taking derivatives, as before,

$$\frac{dM}{dP}\frac{1}{M}\log_e 10 = 2\beta_1(\log_e 10)(\log_{10} P)\frac{1}{P},$$

which yields

$$\frac{dM}{dP}\frac{P}{M} = \text{elasticity of } M \text{ with respect to } P$$

$$= 2\beta_1 \log_{10} P,$$

or, in our particular case,

$$= .062 \log_{10} P.$$

Thus in this model the elasticity of M with respect to P is a slowly increasing function of log P. For countries around 100,000, the elasticity of parliamentary size with respect to population is about .3; for countries of 100,000,000, it is nearly .5. Table 3-7 tabulates the relationship.

TABLE 3-7
Predictions of the Second Model

Population	Log population	Elasticity of M with respect to P = .062 log $_{10}$ P
10,000	4	.248
100,000	5	.310
1,000,000	6	.372
10,000,000	7	.434
100,000,000	8	.496
750,000,000	8.875	.550

The first model assumes that the elasticity is constant and provides an estimate under that untested assumption. The second model assumes that the elasticity varies as the population varies and provides an estimate under that untested assumption. The second is now favored because (1) visual inspection of the scatterplot and the residuals shows a bend in the data and (2) the second explains more variance than the first, even though both models estimate the same number of coefficients.

EXAMPLE 2 FOR THE LOG-LOG CASE: SIZE OF GOVERNMENTAL BUREAUCRACY AND POPULATION SIZE

For the fifty U.S. states, let B = the number of employees of the state government and let P = the number of people living in the state. Both P and B are highly skewed variables, and so we will work with log P and log B. Figure 3-24 shows log B plotted against log P.

Three sorts of general results could emerge from this analysis: (1) if a kind of Parkinson's Law held, then we would expect the bureaucracies of state governments to grow faster than the size of the state; (2) if there were, say, economies of scale, then we would expect bureaucracies to grow more slowly than the population of the state; and (3) the number of bureaucrats could grow in constant proportion to the size of the state. Obviously, other sorts of explanations can be used to explain the results of the analysis. The point here is that the number of employees of the state government can grow

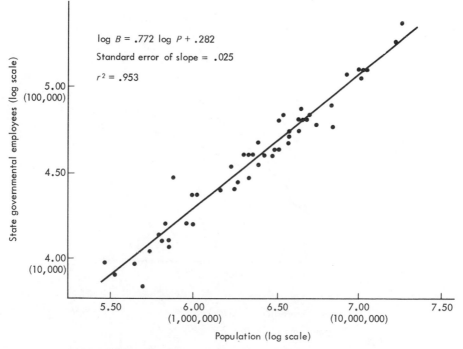

FIGURE 3-24   Population and state government employees

faster, slower, or at the same rate as the number of citizens in the state.

The model that helps to choose among these possibilities is

$$\log B = \beta_1 \log P + \beta_0$$

or, letting $\beta_0 = \log c$ and taking antilogs, puts the model in terms of the untransformed variables:

$$B = cP^{\beta_1}.$$

If β_1 is approximately one, then B approximately equals cP, which says that B grows linearly in direct proportion as P grows. In this case, there is support for what might loosely be called the "null hypothesis" concerning the relationship between size and the dependent variable. An example where β_1 would be very close to one and the null hypothesis accepted would be the relationship between the

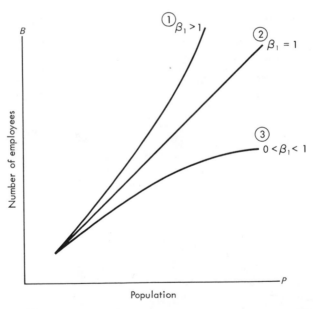

① B grows faster than P
② B grows proportionally to P
③ B grows more slowly than P

FIGURE 3-25   Three types of relationships between B and P

size of the population and the number of women in the population. In this case, given the sex ratio, c would be about .52.

In terms of the untransformed variables, if the estimated regression coefficient is greater than one, the slope increases as P increases. If β_1 lies between zero and one, the slope continually decreases. Figure 3-25 shows this result in a plot of the untransformed variables.

For the fifty states, we have the following results:

$$\log B = .772 \log P + .282,$$

$$\text{Elasticity} = \hat{\beta}_1 = .772,$$

$$\text{Standard error of elasticity} = .025, \qquad r^2 = .953.$$

Figure 3-24 shows the fitted curve.

The estimated elasticity is less than unity, indicating that the number of government employees grows somewhat more slowly than population. A change of one percent in the size of the population of a state is associated with a change of .772 percent in the number of government employees.

Note that the correlation coefficient is virtually useless in this problem. The square of the correlation provides a measure of the goodness of fit; but what is important is the estimate of the slope.

EXAMPLE 3 FOR THE LOG-LOG CASE: TESTING THE "CUBE LAW" RELATING SEATS AND VOTES WITH A LOGIT MODEL

One well-known description of the relationship between votes and seats in two-party systems is the "cube law."[16] The most economical statement of the law is that the cube of the vote odds equals the seat odds, where the vote odds are the ratio of the share of the votes received by one party divided by the share of the votes received by the competing party. For example, if both parties win 50 percent of the votes, then the odds are one to one. Figure 3-26 shows the line traced out by the cube law.

Quite a number of papers have touched upon the law and, in the last few years, the law has enjoyed a certain vogue and has been fitted to electoral outcomes in England, the United States, New Zealand, and, in a modified form, Canada. With one or two exceptions, discussions of the law are quite sympathetic, suggesting that it is

[16]This discussion follows E. R. Tufte, "The Relationship Between Seats and Votes in Two-Party Systems," *American Political Science Review,* 68 (June 1973), 540–54. Additional discussion of the paper is found in the *American Political Science Review,* 68 (March, 1974), 207–13.

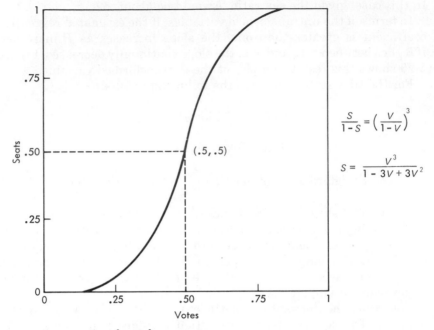

$$\frac{S}{1-S} = \left(\frac{V}{1-V}\right)^3$$

$$S = \frac{V^3}{1 - 3V + 3V^2}$$

S = proportion of seats for one party

$1 - S$ = proportion of seats for the other party
        in a two party system

V = proportion of votes for one party

$1 - V$ = proportion of votes for other party

FIGURE 3–26 The cube law
SOURCE: Figure follows James G. March, "Party Representation as
        a Function of Election Results," *Public Opinion Quarterly*,
        11 (Winter 1957–58), p. 524.

a useful and accurate description of electoral realities. Most studies
consider no more than a few data points and conclude that the law
fits rather well—although the quality of fit is usually assessed
informally and no alternative fits are tried. Let us consider a direct
test of the predictions of the cube law by using the log-log model.
The law is

$$\frac{S}{1-S} = \left(\frac{V}{1-V}\right)^3.$$

The ratio of shares of seats and votes won by the two parties represents the odds that a party will win a seat or a vote. Taking logarithms yields

$$\log_e \frac{S}{1 - S} = 3 \log_e \frac{V}{1 - V},$$

and therefore in the regression of log-odds on seats against log-odds on votes,

$$\log_e \frac{S}{1 - S} = \beta_0 + \beta_1 \log_e \frac{V}{1 - V},$$

the cube law makes the simultaneous joint prediction that $\beta_0 = 0$ and $\beta_1 = 3$. Table 3-8 reports the results of tests of these predictions.

The table indicates that the cube law fits poorly in six of the seven trials. It fits quite well for the last eight elections in Great Britain, but otherwise its predictions are not confirmed. In short, it is not a "law." Since previous studies have not tested the exact joint predictions of the cube law (that is, $\beta_0 = 0$ and $\beta_1 = 3$) or used as extensive a collection of data, these results should be decisive in evaluating the empirical merits of the cube law.

Our previous analysis of seats and votes (Example 4) points to other defects in the cube law. The law hides important political issues because it implies that the translation of votes into seats is (1) unvarying over place and time, and (2) always "fair," in the sense that the curve traced out by the law passes through the point (50 percent votes, 50 percent seats), and the bias is zero.

As we have seen, these implications are not true. The rate of translation of votes into seats differs greatly across political systems, ranging between gains of 1.3 to 3.7 percent in seats for each 1.0 percent gain in votes. Also the results in Table 3-8 indicate that some electoral systems persistently favor a particular party; the votes-seats curve traced out by the data does not inevitably pass close by the point (50 percent votes, 50 percent seats).

The model estimated in the test of the cube law is called a "logit model." Define the odds in favor of a party winning a seat as $S/(1 - S)$ and the vote odds as $V/(1 - V)$. The logit model is the regression of the logarithm of seat odds against the logarithm of vote odds (a regression used earlier to test the specific predictions of the cube law):

TABLE 3-8
Testing the Predictions of the Cube Law (and Simultaneously Estimating
the Logit Model)

	$\hat{\beta}_0$	$\hat{\beta}_1$	Standard error of slope	r^2	Does $\beta_0 = 0$ and $\beta_1 = 3$ as cube law predicts?	Is $\beta_0 \neq 0$; that is, is There a significant bias?
Great Britain	−.02	2.88	.30	.94	Yes	No bias
New Zealand	−.12	2.31	.27	.91	No	Yes, there is a bias
United States, 1868–1970	.09	2.52	.24	.68	No	Yes
United States, 1900–1970	.17	2.20	.15	.86	No	Yes
Michigan	−.17	2.19	.43	.76	No	Yes
New Jersey	−.77	2.09	.59	.29	No	Yes
New York	−.23	1.33	.19	.74	No	Yes

$$\log_e \frac{S}{1 - S} = \beta_0 + \beta_1 \log_e \frac{V}{1 - V}.$$

Since both variables are logged, the estimate of the slope, $\hat{\beta}_1$, is
the estimated elasticity of seat odds with respect to vote odds; that
is, a change of one percent in the vote odds is associated with a
change of $\hat{\beta}_1$ percent in seat odds.

The logit model has the advantage over the linear fit used in Example
4 of producing a reasonable predicted value for the share of seats
for all logically possible values of the share of votes; the predicted
values stay between 0 and 100 percent seats for any percentage share
of votes. As noted earlier, this is only a theoretical virtue, since the
more extreme values do not occur empirically. The logit model also
provides a direct test of the hypothesis that an electoral system is
unbiased, since $\beta_0 = 0$ in an unbiased system. As shown in Table
3-8, there is a statistically significant bias in all cases except Great
Britain.

CASE II—RESPONSE VARIABLE LOGGED, DESCRIBING
VARIABLE NOT LOGGED

Here we have the model of the form

$$\log Y = \beta_0 + \beta_1 X.$$

One particularly interesting application of such a model derives from the exponential:

$$Y = ae^{bX}.$$

Taking natural logarithms and letting $c = \log_e a$ puts this model into the form of case II:

$$\log_e Y = c + bX.$$

This exponential model can be estimated by ordinary least squares, and the regression coefficient has the following interpretation:

In the model $Y = ae^{bX}$, $b \times 100$ is approximately equal to the *percent increase in Y per unit increase in X*, if b is small (say, less than .25).

The proof of this statement relies on the series expansion of e^X:

Percent increase in Y per unit increase in X

$$= \frac{\dfrac{\Delta Y}{Y}}{\Delta X}$$

$$= \frac{Y_2 - Y_1}{Y_1} \qquad (\text{since } \Delta X = X_2 - X_1 = 1)$$

$$= \frac{ae^{bX_2} - ae^{bX_1}}{ae^{bX_1}}$$

$$= e^{(bX_2 - bX_1)} - 1$$

$$= e^b - 1 \quad (\text{since } X_2 - X_1 = 1)$$

$$= [1 + b + \frac{1}{2!} b^2 + \frac{1}{3!} b^3 + \ldots] - 1,$$

by the expansion of e^b. So, if b is small, we can drop the higher-order terms, leaving

$$= (1 + b) - 1 = b.$$

Thus $b \times 100$ equals the percent increase in Y associated with a unit increase in X.[17]

The logarithm of the response variable is used in estimating rates of increase over time. Table 3-10 shows the gross national product of Japan from 1961 to 1970. Note the increasing absolute increase in GNP growth—GNP (the yearly absolute increase) itself increases over time. One process generating such increasing increases is a constant *percentage* growth rate—just like compound interest. What is the appropriate model for a constant percentage growth rate? Consider compound interest, at i percent per year. Beginning the first year with principal P_0 leads to principal P_t after t years:

$$P_t = P_0 (1 + i)^t.$$

For example, after one year:

$$P_1 = P_0(1 + i).$$

After two years

$$P_2 = P_1(1 + i)$$

$$= P_0(1 + i)^2,$$

and so on. To put this into slightly more familiar notation:

$$Y_t = Y_0(1 + i)^t.$$

Taking the logarithm of both sides

$$\log Y_t = \log[Y_0(1 + i)^t],$$

$$\log Y_t = \log Y_0 + \log(1 + i)^t,$$

$$\log Y_t = \log Y_0 + t \log(1 + i).$$

[17] An application of this interpretation is found in Philip E. Sartwell and Charles Anello, "Trends in Mortality from Thromboembolic Disorders," in Advisory Committee on Obstetrics and Gynecology, Food and Drug Administration, *Second Report on the Oral Contraceptives* (Washington, D.C.: U.S. Government Printing Office, 1969), 37–39.

Now let

$$\beta_0 = \log Y_0,$$

$$\beta_1 = \log(1 + i),$$

and we have the model

$$\log Y_t = \beta_0 + \beta_1 t$$

—that is, case II. The model is estimated by letting $Y = \log Y_t$, yielding

$$Y = \beta_0 + \beta_1 t,$$

the usual linear model.

Figure 3-27 shows the GNP of Japan plotted on both an absolute scale and a logarithmic scale. Note how, for these data, the log scale throws the data points into a straight line. The changes in the logarithm of GNP are relatively constant (Table 3-9), indicating a relatively constant percentage rate of growth over time. The line for log GNP fits considerably better than the line for absolute GNP—as the r^2 shows. The fitted line for the logarithmic case is

$$\log_{10} \text{GNP} = 1.627 + .064\,t.$$

The rate of growth, i, can be estimated by going back to the original linearization of the model,

$$\beta_1 = \log(1 + i),$$

and solving by taking antilogarithms. This yields

$$\hat{i} = .159,$$

or a growth rate of almost 16 percent per year.[18]

This is the yearly rate of growth. An instantaneous rate of growth can be estimated by fitting the model

---

[18]Unfortunately the estimate, $\hat{i}$, is biased. It does not have least-squares properties because the sum of squares was minimized with respect to log GNP rather than GNP over time.

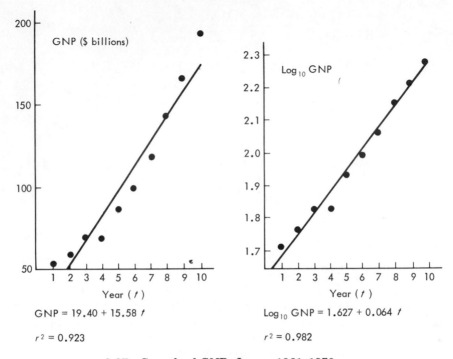

FIGURE **3-27**   Growth of GNP, Japan, 1961–1970

$$\log_e Y = \beta_0 + \beta_1 t.$$

Differentiating gives

$$\beta_1 = \frac{dY/Y}{dt},$$

the percentage rate of growth in Y.

Finally, a growth rate can be estimated quite soundly without the regression model, simply by taking the average (mean, median, or midmean) of the yearly growth rates, or the average of the logarithm.

CASE III—RESPONSE VARIABLE UNLOGGED, DESCRIBING
VARIABLE LOGGED

The model is

$$Y = \beta_0 + \beta_1 \log X.$$

TABLE 3-9

Gross National Product, Japan, 1961–1970

Year	t	GNP ($ Billion)	Yearly increase in GNP	log_{10} GNP	Yearly increase in log^{10} GNP
1961	1	53		1.72	
			6		.05
1962	2	59		1.77	
			9		.06
1963	3	68		1.83	
			0		.00
1964	4	68		1.83	
			17		.10
1965	5	85		1.93	
			12		.06
1966	6	97		1.99	
			19		.07
1967	7	116		2.06	
			26		.09
1968	8	142		2.15	
			24		.07
1969	9	166		2.22	
			31		.08
1970	10	197		2.30	

If the logarithm of the describing variable is taken to the base 10, the regression indicates that a change in the order of magnitude of X—that is, a tenfold increase in X—is associated with a change of β_1 units in Y.

Sometimes it is useful to take the logarithm to the base 2 in this model. In such a case, the regression coefficient estimates the increase in Y when X doubles. And so when X is measured with respect to time, the estimate of the regression coefficient may be said to assess the "doubling time" of Y with respect to X. It is easy to prove that when X doubles, Y increases by β_1 units. The model is

$$Y = \beta_0 + \beta_1 \log_2 X.$$

Now suppose X doubles:

$$Y_{new} = \beta_0 + \beta_1 \log_2 2X$$

$$= \beta_0 + \beta_1(\log_2 2 + \log_2 X)$$

$$= \beta_0 + \beta_1 \log_2 X + \beta_1$$

$$= Y + \beta_1$$

—that is, the value of Y after X doubles is the old value of Y plus β_1. Thus Y increases by β_1 units when X doubles.

Consider the following application of this model. Kelley and Mirer have developed a rule predicting how voters will vote; the predictions are made on the basis of an interview with the voter D days before the election. After the election, the voter is reinterviewed and asked how he or she voted. Thus it is possible to find the rate of error in prediction—and such errors might well be related to how many days before the election the voter was interviewed. If D were 1000 days, to take an extreme example, the error rate in prediction would be higher than if D were one day. The researchers analyzed the data first with a linear model, then with a logarithmic model:

A simple linear regression of the first of these variables on the second shows them to be strongly related. The equation yielded is:

rate of error = 17.4 + .23(days before election).

In a statistical sense this relationship explains some 28 percent of the variance in the dependent variable, and, since the standard error of the estimated coefficient is .07, the relationship is statistically significant ($t = 3.15$). Most interesting, perhaps, is the implication of the equation's constant term: Had the interviews of these respondents been conducted on election day, the mean rate of error in predicting their votes would have been 17.4 percent. . . .

And it is quite possible that this value for the constant term is too high. The volume of partisan propaganda is normally much heavier in the last two or three weeks of a presidential campaign than it is earlier. We might therefore suppose the relationship between time and changes of opinion to be like that shown in Figure [3-28], in which the likelihood of such changes (and thus the error rates of our predictions) at first increases rapidly with increases in the number of days between election day and the time the opinions were expressed, then more slowly. By regressing the rates of error in our predictions for groups of respondents on the logarithm (to the base 2) of the mean number of days before election day that the respondents in each group were interviewed, one can see if a curve like that shown in Figure [3-28] fits the data that entered into the first regression. The equation produced by this new regression is:

rate of error = 5.3 + 4.03($\log_2$ days before election).

This second equation accounts for as much of the variance in the dependent variable as did the first and yields an equally reliable estimate of the regression coefficient ($r^2 = .28$, $t = 3.14$). The value of the equation's constant term implies that our mean rate of error in predicting the votes of groups of respondents would have been 5.3 percent . . . if those respondents had been interviewed one day

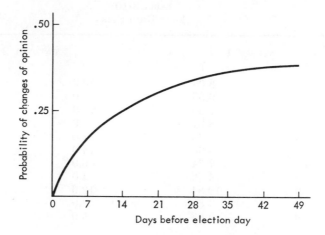

FIGURE 3-28   Hypothetical relationship between the likelihood that opinions will change and the time that attitudes toward parties and candidates are expressed

before election day. The equation as a whole implies that, starting from the day before the election, the error rate in predictions derived from the Rule will rise by four percentage points with each doubling of the length of time before election day that respondents are interviewed.[19]

Example 7: Regressions Aren't Enough— Looking at the Scatterplot

F. J. Anscombe has constructed a nice set of numbers illustrating why it is important to look at scatterplots along with the fitted equation.[20] Table 3-10 shows four sets of data. Their remarkable property is that all four yield exactly the same result when a linear model is fitted. The regression in all four cases is:

$$Y = 3.0 + .5X,$$

$r^2 = .667$, estimated standard error of $\beta_1 = 0.118$,

[19]Stanley Kelley, Jr., and Thad W. Mirer, "The Simple Act of Voting," *American Political Science Review*, 68 (June, 1974).

[20]F. J. Anscombe, "Graphs in Statistical Analysis," *American Statistician*, 27 (February 1973), 17–21.

TABLE **3-10**
Four Data Sets

DATA SET 1		DATA SET 2	
X	Y	X	Y
10.0	8.04	10.0	9.14
8.0	6.95	8.0	8.14
13.0	7.58	13.0	8.74
9.0	8.81	9.0	8.77
11.0	8.33	11.0	9.26
14.0	9.96	14.0	8.10
6.0	7.24	6.0	6.13
4.0	4.26	4.0	3.10
12.0	10.84	12.0	9.13
7.0	4.82	7.0	7.26
5.0	5.68	5.0	4.74

DATA SET 3		DATA SET 4	
X	Y	X	Y
10.0	7.46	8.0	6.58
8.0	6.77	8.0	5.76
13.0	12.74	8.0	7.71
9.0	7.11	8.0	8.84
11.0	7.81	8.0	8.47
14.0	8.84	8.0	7.04
6.0	6.08	8.0	5.25
4.0	5.39	19.0	12.50
12.0	8.15	8.0	5.56
7.0	6.42	8.0	7.91
5.0	5.73	8.0	6.89

SOURCE: F. J. Anscombe, *op. cit.*

mean of $X = 9.0$,

mean of $Y = 7.5$, for all four data sets.

And yet the four situations—although numerically equivalent in major respects—are substantively very different. Figure 3-29 shows how very different the four data sets actually are.

Anscombe has emphasized the importance of visual displays in statistical analysis:

> Most textbooks on statistical methods, and most statistical computer programs, pay too little attention to graphs. Few of us escape being indoctrinated with these notions:

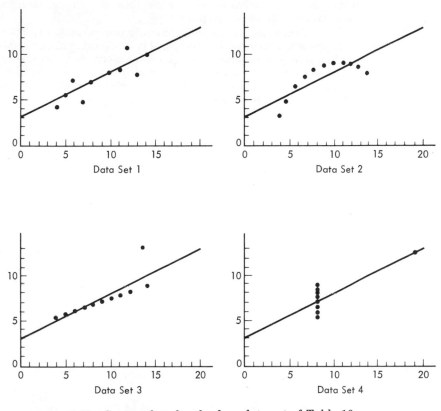

FIGURE 3-29 Scatterplots for the four data set of Table 10
SOURCE: F. J. Anscombe, *op. cit.*

(1) numerical calculations are exact, but graphs are rough;

(2) for any particular kind of statistical data there is just one set of calculations constituting a correct statistical analysis;

(3) performing intricate calculations is virtuous, whereas actually looking at the data is cheating.

A computer should make *both* calculations *and* graphs. Both sorts of output should be studied; each will contribute to understanding.

Graphs can have various purposes, such as: (i) to help us perceive and appreciate some broad features of the data, (ii) to let us look behind those broad features and see what else is there. Most kinds of statistical calculation rest on assumptions about the behavior of the data. Those assumptions may be false, and then the calculations may be misleading. We ought always to try to check whether the assumptions are reasonably correct; and if they are wrong we ought to be able to perceive in what ways they are wrong. Graphs are very valuable for these purposes.[21]

Up until now we have considered only one-variable explanations of the response variable. But the world is surely often more complicated than that and response variables have more than a single cause. In the next chapter, we examine the *multiple regression* model which allows us to take into account effectively several explanatory variables—at least some of the time.

---

[21] Anscombe, *op. cit.*, p. 17.

CHAPTER 4

Multiple Regression

"Some circumstantial evidence is very strong, as when you find a trout in the milk."

—Henry David Thoreau

The Model

In chapter 3 we estimated the two-variable model,

Loss by President's
party in midterm $= \beta_0 + \beta_1$ (presidential
congressional elections   approval rating),

and decided that a more elaborate model would help explain additional variation in the response variable. The more elaborate version used two describing variables, presidential approval and economic conditions:

vote loss $= \beta_0 + \beta_1$ (presidential $+ \beta_2$ (economic
                   approval)   conditions).

Just as in the two-variable case, we can use the data to estimate the three parameters of this model:

1. the constant term, β_0,
2. the regression coefficient for presidential popularity, β_1,
3. the regression coefficient for economic conditions, β_2.

135

And, as before, the parameters are estimated by least squares, minimizing the sum of the squared deviations of the observed value from the fitted value:

$$\text{minimize}\quad \Sigma\,(Y_i - \hat{Y}_i)^2$$

This is the multiple regression model. We can have more than two describing variables: the general multiple regression model with K describing variables is

$$Y = \beta_0 + \beta_1 X_1 + \beta_2 X_2 + \cdots + \beta_k X_k.$$

The causal model behind multiple regression is that there are k multiple, independent causes of Y, the response variable:

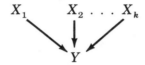

This is a somewhat limited model, since it excludes estimates of links *between* the describing variables—for example,

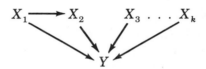

Also simple multiple regression models do not estimate feedback relationships:

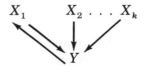

Under some circumstances, models involving feedback and simultaneous relationships can be estimated.

Multiple regression is widely used in the study of economics, politics, and policy. It allows the inclusion of many describing variables in a convenient framework. It is a carefully investigated and fairly widely understood statistical procedure; thus it is a relatively effective way to communicate the results of a multivariate analysis. And packages for running multiple regressions are available with most every computer.

Almost all of the technical apparatus used in the two-variable model applies to the multivariate case. Consider the three-variable model:

$$Y = \beta_0 + \beta_1 X_1 + \beta_2 X_2.$$

We use the data to compute:

1. the estimated regression coefficients, $\hat{\beta}_0$, $\hat{\beta}_1$, and $\hat{\beta}_2$;
2. their standard errors, $S_{\hat{\beta}_1}$, $S_{\hat{\beta}_2}$;
3. t-values to test for statistical significance of the coefficients, $\hat{\beta}_1/S_{\hat{\beta}_1}$, $\hat{\beta}_2/S_{\hat{\beta}_2}$;
4. the ratio of explained variation to total variation, R^2.

The estimated coefficients of the model generate the predicted values

$$\hat{Y}_i = \hat{\beta}_0 + \hat{\beta}_1 X_{1i} + \hat{\beta}_2 X_{2i},$$

where X_{1i} and X_{2i} are the observed values of X_1 and X_2, respectively, for the ith case. Now, since we have an observed and a predicted value for each observation, the residuals are defined as usual, measured along the Y axis:

$$Y_i - \hat{Y}_i,$$

and $\Sigma (Y_i - \hat{Y}_i)^2$ is minimized in the estimates of β_0, β_1, and β_2. No other set of $\hat{\beta}_0$, $\hat{\beta}_1$, and $\hat{\beta}_2$ will make the sum of the squared deviations smaller. As in the two-variable case, the principle of least squares generates the estimating equations for the coefficients. And, as in the two-variable case, a variety of assumptions about the data are required for the sound application of statistical significance testing in the model.[1]

The percentage of the variance explained statistically is also analogous to the two-variable case:

$$R^2 = \frac{\text{explained variation}}{\text{total variation}} = \frac{\Sigma (\hat{Y}_i - \bar{Y})^2}{\Sigma (Y_i - \bar{Y})^2}.$$

[1] See Ronald J. Wonnacott and Thomas H. Wonnacott, *Econometrics* (New York: Wiley, 1970); J. Johnston, *Econometric Methods,* 2d ed. (New York: McGraw-Hill, 1972); or other statistics or econometrics texts for discussion of the assumptions.

Since the R^2 provides some measure of the quality of overall fit of the describing variables in predicting Y, it is sometimes used to choose between different regressions containing different combinations of describing variables.

R can also be interpreted as the simple corrrelation between the observed and predicted values; that is,

$$R = r_{Y\hat{Y}}.$$

The estimated regression coefficients in a multiple regression are interpreted as *partial slopes*. They try to answer the question: When X_k, the kth describing variable, changes by one unit and all the other describing variables are held constant (in a statistical sense), how much change is expected in Y? The answer is β_k units. If the describing variables were completely unrelated to one another, then the regression coefficients in the multiple regression would be the same as if each describing variable were regressed one at a time on Y. However, the describing variables are inevitably interrelated, and thus all the coefficients in the model are estimated and examined in combination.

Two different types of regression coefficients—unstandardized and standardized—are used in practice. Unstandardized coefficients are interpreted in the units of measurement in which the variables are measured; for example, a one percent change in votes is associated with a β_1 percent change in seats. Standardized coefficients rescale all the variables into standard deviations from the mean:

$$\frac{Y_i - \bar{Y}}{S_Y}, \; \frac{X_{1i} - \bar{X}_1}{S_{X_1}}, \; \frac{X_{2i} - \bar{X}_2}{S_{X_2}}, \; \dots \; .$$

Thus, in the standardized case, all variables are expressed in the same units—that is, in standard deviations. Standardized regression coefficients are analogous to the correlation coefficient in the two-variable case; unstandardized coefficients are analogous to the slope in the two-variable case. Standardized coefficients are useful when the natural scale of measurement does not have a particularly meaningful interpretation or when some relative comparison of the variables with respect to their standard deviations is needed. All the examples presented here use unstandardized regression coefficients.

The regression coefficients gain their meaning from the substance of the problem at hand. The statistical model merely provides the answer to the question: *Under the assumption that X_i is a cause* *of* Y, what is the expected change in Y for a unit change in X? Thus the estimating procedure *assumes* the causal model:

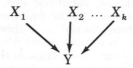

Whether or not there really is a causal relationship between Y and $X_1, X_2, ..., X_k$ depends on having a theory, consistent with the data, that links the variables. And in trying to assess the independent effect of one of the describing variables on Y by "holding constant" or "adjusting out" all the other describing variables, we must always keep in mind that the "holding constant" or "adjusting out" is done *statistically,* by the manipulation of the observed data. The variables are passively observed; we are not really intervening in the system and holding constant all variables except one. And so the causal structure of the multiple regression model is not strongly tested by the statistical control, adjustment, or holding constant of the variables. George Box soundly described the contrast between the statistical control of observed variables and the actual experimental control (and deliberate manipulation) of variables: "To find out what happens to a system when you interfere with it, you have to interfere with it (not just passively observe it)."[2]

Still, in many cases in political and policy analysis, the best we can do in trying to understand what is going on is to hold constant or control variables statistically rather than experimentally—for there is simply no other way to investigate many important questions.

Example 1: Midterm Congressional Elections Presidential Popularity and Economic Conditions

In every midterm congressional election but one since the Civil War, the political party of the incumbent President has lost seats in the House of Representatives. This persistent outcome results from differences in turnout in midterm compared to on-year elections:

> Explanation of the Administration's loss at midterm must be sought not so much by examining the midterm election itself as by looking

[2]Quoted in John P. Gilbert and Frederick Mosteller, "The Urgent Need for Experimentation," in Frederick Mosteller and Daniel P. Moynihan, eds., *On Equality of Education Opportunity* (New York: Vintage, 1972), p. 372.

at the preceding presidential election. The stimulation of the presidential campaign brings a relatively large turnout. It attracts to the polls persons of low political interest who in large degree support the winning presidential candidate and, incidentally, his party's congressional candidates. At the following midterm congressional election, turnout drops sharply. . . . Those who stay home include in special degree the in-and-out voters who had helped the President and his congressional ticket into office. As they remain on the sidelines at midterm, the President's allies in marginal districts may find themselves voted from office. The coattail vote of the preceding presidential year that edged these Representatives into office simply stays at home . . .[3]

Yet this view of midterm elections is incomplete—for it only explains why the President's party should almost always be operating in the loss column rather than accounting for the *amount* of votes lost by the President's party. In statistical parlance, what has been explained is the location of the mean rather than variability about the mean. In studying the variability about the mean, we seek to answer such questions as: Why do some Presidents lose fewer congressional seats at the midterm than other Presidents? What factors affect the magnitude of the loss of congressional seats by the President's party? In Chapter 3, we used a two-variable regression to begin to answer these questions; however, that model left some variability unexplained. A more complicated model, bringing in the effect of economic conditions on the election, appears useful.

In order to explain the magnitude of the loss of votes and congressional seats by the President's party in midterm elections, we will estimate the following multiple regression model:

$$\begin{array}{l} \text{Votes loss by} \\ \text{President's party} \end{array} = \beta_0 + \beta_1 \begin{bmatrix} \text{Presidential} \\ \text{popularity} \end{bmatrix} + \beta_2 \begin{bmatrix} \text{Economic} \\ \text{conditions} \end{bmatrix}$$

The idea is, then, that the lower the approval rating of the incumbent President and the less prosperous the economy, the greater the loss of support for the President's party in the midterm congressional elections. Thus the model assumes that voters, in midterm elections, reward or punish the political party of the President on the basis of their evaluation of (1) the performance of the President in general and (2) his management of the economy in particular.

[3] V. O. Key, *Politics, Parties, and Pressure Groups*, 5th ed. (New York: Thomas Y. Crowell, 1964), pp. 568–69.

The model is:

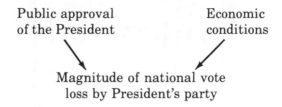

Public approval
of the President

Economic
conditions

Magnitude of national vote
loss by President's party

Three variables must be measured. With respect to economic conditions, recent studies of the relationship between aggregate economic conditions and the outcome of congressional elections show that interelection shifts of ordinary magnitude in unemployment have less impact on congressional elections than do shifts in real income.[4] Thus the most meaningful measure of economic conditions for our model appears to be the interelection change in real disposable income per capita. This measure probably may reflect the economic concerns of most voters, for it assesses the short-run shift in the average economic conditions prevailing at the individual level—a shift in conditions for which some voters might hold the incumbent administration responsible.

For this model, the public's evaluation of the President's general performance is measured by the standard Gallup Poll question: "Do you approve or disapprove of the way President____is handling his job as President?" Table 4-1 shows responses to the survey taken each September prior to the midterm election.

The most important variable to measure well is the magnitude of the vote loss by the President's party. The idea of "loss" implies the question "Relative to what?" The relevant comparison is between the normal, long-run congressional vote for the political party of the current President and the outcome of the midterm election at hand—that is, a standardized vote loss:

$$
\begin{pmatrix} \text{standardized vote} \\ \text{loss by President's} \\ \text{party in the } i\text{th} \\ \text{midterm election} \end{pmatrix} = \begin{pmatrix} \text{average vote for} \\ \text{party of current} \\ \text{President in the} \\ \text{last 8 elections} \end{pmatrix} - \begin{pmatrix} \text{vote for} \\ \text{President's} \\ \text{party in the} \\ i\text{th election} \end{pmatrix}
$$

The loss is measured with respect to how well the party of the current

[4]Gerald H. Kramer, "Short-Term Fluctuations in U.S. Voting Behavior, 1896–1964," *American Political Science Review*, 65 (March 1971), 131–43; George J. Stigler, "General Economic Conditions and National Elections," *American Economic Review Papers and Proceedings*, 63 (May 1973), 160–67 and further discussion, 169–80.

TABLE 4-1
The Data

Year	Mean congressional vote for party of current President in last 8 elections		Nationwide congressional vote for party of current President	Standardized vote loss	Gallup Poll rating of President at time of election	Current yearly change in real disposable income per capita
1946	Democratic	52.57%	45.27%	7.30%	32%	−$36
1950	Democratic	52.04%	50.04%	2.00%	43%	$99
1954	Republican	49.79%	47.46%	2.33%	65%	−$12
1958	Republican	49.83%	43.91%	5.92%	56%	−$13
1962	Democratic	51.63%	52.42%	−.79%	67%	$60
1966	Democratic	53.06%	51.33%	1.73%	48%	$96
1970	Republican	46.66%	45.68%	.98%	56%	$69

President has normally tended to do, where the normal vote is computed by averaging that party's vote over the eight preceding congressional elections. This standardization is necessary because the Democrats have dominated postwar congressional elections; thus, if the unstandardized vote won by the President's party is used as the response (dependent) variable, the Republican presidents would appear to do poorly. For example, when the Republicans win 48 percent of the national congressional vote, it is, relatively, a substantial victory for that party and should be measured as such. The eight-election normalization takes this effect into account.

Table 4.1 shows the data matrix for the postwar midterm elections. We now consider the multiple regression fitting these data.

Table 4.2 shows the estimates of the model's coefficients. The results are statistically secure, since the coefficients are several times their standard errors. The fitted equation indicates:

1. A change in Presidential popularity of 10 percentage points in the Gallup Poll is associated with a national change of 1.3 percentage points in national midterm votes for congressional candidates of the President's party.
2. A change of $100 in real disposable personal income per capita in the year prior to the midterm election is associated with a national change of 3.5 percentage points in midterm votes for congressional candidates of the President's party.

The fitted equation explains statistically 89.1 percent of the variance in national midterm election outcomes; or, to put it another way, the correlation between the actual election results and those predicted by the model is .944. Since the fitted equation uses two meaningful explanatory variables, it seems reasonable to believe in this case

TABLE 4-2
Multiple Regression Fitting Standardized Vote Loss by
President's Party in Midterm Elections

		Regression coefficient and (standard error)
β_1	Presidential approval rating (Gallup Poll, two months before election)	−.133 (.038)
β_2	Inter-election change in real disposable personal income per capita	−.035 (.015)

$\beta_0 = 11.083$, $R^2 = .891$.

that a successful statistical explanation is also a successful substantive explanation.

The multiple regression model is an equation, weighting the particular values (prevailing in a given election) of Presidential popularity and economic conditions. Thus the recipe for predicting the midterm outcome is to take .133 of the percent approving the President and .035 of the recent change in disposable personal income, subtract all this from β_0 (which is 11.083) and this gives the predicted shift in the midterm vote. Let us see how the equation worked for 1970. The equation, as shown in Table 4-2, fitted to the data is:

$$\text{standardized vote loss} = 11.083 - .133 \left(\begin{array}{c}\text{Percent approving}\\\text{President}\end{array}\right) - .035 \left(\begin{array}{c}\text{Change in}\\\text{income}\end{array}\right)$$

For 1970, the percent approving the President was 56 percent; the change in disposable personal income per capita was $69. Putting these particular values in the weighted combination of the regression yields:

$$
\begin{aligned}
\text{standardized vote loss predicted for 1970} &= 11.083 - .133\,(56) - .035\,(69)\\
&= 11.083 - 7.448 - 2.415\\
&= 1.2
\end{aligned}
$$

As Table 4-1 shows, the actual standardized vote loss for 1970 was 1.0, and thus the model fits the data rather well for 1970. As usual, the residual is the observed minus the predicted value; and thus the residual for 1970 from the fitted regression is −0.2.

As another check of the adequacy of the model, its predictions of midterm outcomes were compared with those made by the Gallup Poll in the national survey conducted a week to ten days before each election. As Table 4-3 shows, the model outperforms, in six of seven elections, the pre-election predictions based on surveys directly asking voters how they intend to vote. All this, of course, is after the fact; it would be more useful to have a prediction in hand prior to the election to test the model.

An analysis based on so few data points (N = 7 elections) can be very sensitive to outlying values in the data. In order to test

TABLE 4-3
After-the-Fact Predictive Error of the Model

Year	Actual vote for House candidates, President's party	Gallup Poll prediction	Model prediction	Gallup absolute error	Model absolute error
1946	45.3	42	44.5	3.3	.8
1950	50.0	51	50.2	1.0	.2
1954	47.5	48.5	46.9	1.1	.6
1958	43.9	43	45.6	.9	1.7
1962	52.4	55.5	51.6	3.1	.8
1966	51.3	52.5	51.8	1.2	.5
1970	45.7	47	45.5	1.3	.2

Average absolute error, Gallup = 1.7 percentage points
Average absolute error, Model = 0.7 percentage points

the stability of the fitted equation, the multiple regression was recomputed after omitting one election at a time. Table 4–4 shows the results; even when the regression is based on six elections, the regression coefficients remain fairly stable. The greatest shift occurs when the outlying values for 1946 (very low Presidential approval ratings and a decline in real disposable income per capita in the early postwar period) are dropped from the estimation.

Does the strong aggregate responsiveness of midterm outcomes to economic conditions and evaluations of the President's performance indicate anything about the rationality of the electorate—or about , at least, that half of the eligible citizenry turns out in off-year elections?[5] Such is the usual line of argument, for how else does one explain the choice of variables in the model and the ultimate results? It is important to realize, however, that all we are seeing in these data (and in the many similar studies) is the totally *aggregated* evidence that speaks only most indirectly to what must be the central political questions concerning the rationality of *individual* voters:

1. Do some voters make more rational calculations than others? Which voters? How many?
2. What are the components of these calculations?
3. What kinds of decision rules do individual voters use? Which voters use what decision rules?
4. What conditions encourage voter rationality?
5. How may these conditions be nurtured?

[5] Angus Campbell, "Voters and Elections: Past and Present," *Journal of Politics,* 26 (November 1964), 745–57.

TABLE 4-4

Re-estimating the Regression Coefficients When the Data Points are
Omitted One at a Time

Year omitted	Constant term	Presidential popularity	Change in economic conditions	R^2
1946	17.62	−.23	−.052	.94
1950	10.93	−.13	−.036	.89
1954	10.57	−.12	−.038	.90
1958	11.10	−.15	−.028	.99
1962	10.11	−.11	−.034	.88
1966	10.87	−.13	−.037	.89
1970	11.06	−.13	−.035	.88

Thus, although the results are impressive in terms of the large R^2, there are still substantial inferential problems in trying to interpret the meaning of the model—since the data do not speak directly to the explanatory mechanism postulated to explain the findings.

Let us consider the steps in the construction of this regression in order to look at some of the broader issues in constructing explanatory models. The steps were these:

1. A model, based on prior research and some general ideas, was specified. The model included two basic variables, presidential popularity and economic conditions. There were also several other variables that were candidates for inclusion in the model: whether the nation was involved in a war at the time of the election, the magnitude of the victory of the President's party in the preceding election, and a few others.

2. Each variable in the model was operationalized; that is, a numerical measure for the concept was found. The construction of appropriate measures required some further thought, especially with respect to the response variable, the standardized vote.

3. Several economic variables were included in the initial analysis— changes in unemployment, inflation, GNP per capita, and real disposable personal income per capita. From the beginning, the change in real disposable personal income per capita made the most substantive sense, and it turned out that it led to the most successful explanatory model in terms of variance explained. A variety of different regressions were computed.

There is, then, an interplay between explanatory ideas and the examination of the data. Some variables were tried out on the basis of a vague idea and were then discarded when they yielded no explanatory return. For example, some regressions included a variable indicating whether the nation was involved in a war (Korea or Vietnam) during the midterm congressional election—on the hypothesis that there might be a "rally round the flag" effect helping the President. Such appeared to be the case—and the sign of the regression coefficient was in the expected direction—but the results just did not seem solid enough to warrant inclusion in the final model, especially since there are only seven data points and also since only two explanatory variables do so well.

Now, looking at several different multiple regressions and sorting around through different variables may not fit some abstract models of scientific research procedure—but it is normally done in constructing explanatory models, and it is precisely this sorting through of various notions that is the heart of data analysis. The final model reported here has gained inferential strength as a consequence of this directed search through a variety of ideas because the model has been tested against many other alternative possibilities and has survived. The strength of such an interplay between theory and data has been strongly put by Jacob Viner:

> If there is agreement that relevance is of supreme importance for economic theory, it leads to certain rules of guidance as to the procedure we should follow in constructing our theoretical models. It is common practice to start with the simplest and the most rigorous model, and to leave it to a later stage, or to others, to introduce into the model additional variables or other complicating elements. I venture to suggest that the most useful type of "first approximation" would often be of a radically different character. It would consist of a listing of all the variables known or believed to be or suspected of being of substantial significance, and corresponding listing of types and directions of interrelationship between these variables. A second stage of analysis would consist of a combing out on the basis of such empirical evidence as can be accumulated of the probably least significant variables and interrelationships between variables. Instead of beginning with rigor and elegance, only from this second stage on would these become legitimate goals, and even then for a time they should be distant goals, to be given high value only after it is clear that they can be reached without substantial loss of relevance.
>
> Such procedure, it would seem to me, would have some distinct advantages as compared to the more usual procedure on the part of theorists of starting—and often ending—with models that gain their rigor at the cost of unrealistic simplification. In the first case, important variables would be less likely to be omitted from consideration because of oversight, traditional practice, difficulty of manipulation, or unsuitability for specific types of analytical manipulation to which the researcher has an irrational attachment. Secondly, there would be at least partial awareness of what variables had been omitted from the final analysis, and therefore greater likelihood than at present that the conclusions will be offered with the qualifications

and the caution that such omission makes appropriate. Third, if the presentation of the final results includes a statement with respect to the omitted variables and the reasons for their omission, the reader of such presentation is in better position to appraise the significance of the findings and is afforded some measure of guidance as to the further information and the new or improved techniques of analysis that would be most helpful.

The final outcome of such a change in analytical procedure might well be a definite loss in rigor and elegance at least for a long time, on the one hand, but a definite gain in scope for the useful exploitation of new information and of wisdom and insight on the other hand. Such a result, I hope and believe, would in most cases constitute a new gain in relevance for understanding of reality and for the promotion of economic welfare by means of economic theorizing.[6]

Example 2: Equality of Educational Opportunity and Multicollinearity

Modern statisticians are familiar with the notions that any finite body of data contains only a limited amount of information, on any point under examination: that this limit is set by the nature of the data themselves, and cannot be increased by any amount of ingenuity expended in their statistical examination: that the statistician's task, in fact, is limited to the extraction of the whole of the available information on any particular issue.[7]

—R. A. Fisher

If two or more describing variables in an analysis are highly intercorrelated, it will be difficult and perhaps impossible to assess accurately their independent impacts on the response variable. As the association between two or more describing variables grows stronger, it becomes more and more difficult to tell one variable from the other. This problem, called "multicollinearity" in the statistical jargon, sometimes causes difficulties in the analysis of nonexperimental data.

For example, if, in Chapter 1, density and inspections (the two describing variables for the response variable of traffic fatalities) were highly associated—say, all states above a certain density had inspections and all below did not—then it would be very difficult to discover if inspections made a difference because the effect of inspections would be confounded with the effect of density. The

---

[6] Jacob Viner, "International Trade Theory and Its Present Day Relevance," in Brookings Lectures, 1954, *Economics and the Public Policy.* © 1955 by the Brookings Institution, Washington, D.C., pp. 128–30.

[7] R. A. Fisher, *The Design of Experiments,* 8th ed. (London: Oliver and Boyd, 1966), p. 40.

scatterplot, in this hypothetical example, would resemble Figure 4-1. In such a case there is insufficient independent variation in the two describing variables; in particular, there is a shortage of thickly populated states without inspections and thinly populated states with inspections. Without such conditions prevailing in at least a few states, the independent effect of inspections and the independent effect of density on the death rate could not be assessed.

Sometimes clusters of variables tend to vary together in the normal course of events, thereby rendering it difficult to discover the magnitude of the independent effects of the different variables in the cluster. And yet it may be most desirable, from a practical as well as scientific point of view, to disentangle correlated describing variables in order to discover more effective policies to improve conditions. Many economic indicators tend to move together in response to underlying economic and political events. Or consider a research design seeking to assess the effects of air pollution on the health of a city's residents. Such a study might be based on three areas in a city—one with badly polluted air, one with moderate pollution, and (if it could be found) one with relatively clean air. But chances are that the poor are more likely to find housing only in those unpleasant parts of

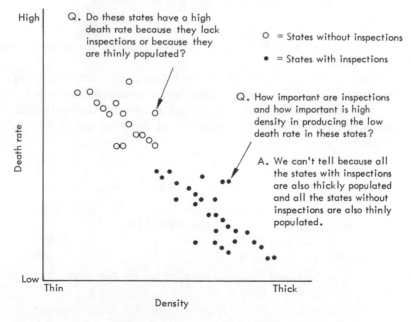

FIGURE 4-1 Hypothetical data showing collinearity between density and inspections

the city near factories and highways producing very polluted air; the moderately polluted area is more likely to be the home of those with moderate incomes; and the wealthy will be concentrated in areas relatively free of pollution. In such a situation, then, the effects of air pollution on health are confounded with the effects of income and housing on health.

The problem of multicollinearity involves a lack of data, a lack of information. In the first example, there were no *thinly* populated states *with* inspections (and vice versa); in the study of the health effects of air pollution, we lacked information about rich neighborhoods with polluted air and poor areas with fresh air.

Recognition of multicollinearity as a lack of information has two important consequences:

1. In order to alleviate the problem, it is necessary to collect more data—especially on the rarer combinations of the describing variables.
2. No statistical technique can go very far to remedy the problem because the fault lies basically with the data rather than the method of analysis. Multicollinearity weakens inferences based on *any* statistical method—regression, path analysis, causal modeling, or cross-tabulations (where the difficulty shows up as a lack of deviant cases and near-empty cells).

Figure 4-2 shows how, when two describing variables are highly intercorrelated, a control for one variable reduces the range of variation in the other.

Since multicollinearity affects our ability to assess the independent influence of each describing variable, its consequences in the multiple regression model include increased errors in the estimate of the regression coefficients. The variance of the estimate of the regression coefficient, $\hat{\beta}_i$, is given by:

$$\text{variance of } \hat{\beta}_i = \frac{1}{N - n - 1} \frac{S_Y^2}{S_{X_i}^2} \frac{1 - R_Y^2}{1 - R_{X_i}^2},$$

where N = number of observations,

      n = number of describing variables,

      S_Y^2 = variance of Y,

      $S_{X_i}^2$ = variance of X_i,

      R_Y^2 = squared multiple correlation for the regression
            $Y = \beta_0 + \beta_1 X_1 + ... + \beta_n X_n$,

      $R_{X_i}^2$ = squared multiple correlation for the regression
            $X_i = \beta_0' + \beta_i' X_i + ... + \beta_{i-1}' X_{i-1} + \beta_{i+1}' X_{i+1} + ...$
            $+ \beta_n' X_n$

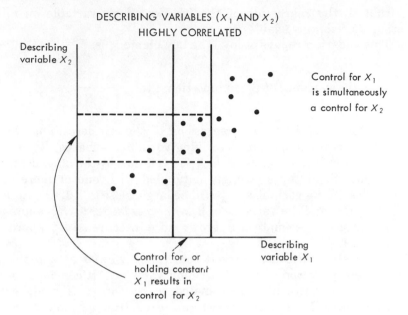

DESCRIBING VARIABLES (X_1 AND X_2)
HIGHLY CORRELATED

Describing variable X_2

Control for X_1
is simultaneously
a control for X_2

Describing variable X_1

Control for, or
holding constant
X_1 results in
control for X_2

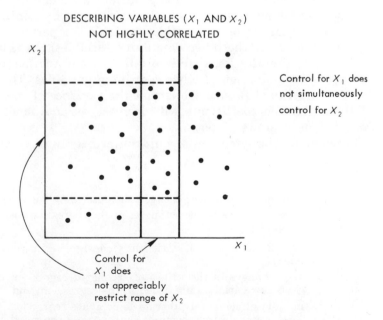

DESCRIBING VARIABLES (X_1 AND X_2)
NOT HIGHLY CORRELATED

X_2

Control for X_1 does
not simultaneously
control for X_2

X_1

Control for
X_1 does
not appreciably
restrict range of X_2

FIGURE 4-2   Effect of controlling for a variable when describing
variables are strongly correlated

—that is, the regression of the ith *describing* variable on all the other *describing* variables.

This equation repays study. The key element is:

$$\text{the variance of } \hat{\beta}_i \text{ is proportional to } \frac{1}{1 - R^2_{X_i}}.$$

Now $R^2_{X_i}$ is the R^2 for the regression of the ith describing variable on all the other remaining describing variables—that is, $R^2_{X_i}$ assesses how well the describing variable X_i is explained by the *other* describing variables. So if X_i is strongly entangled with one or more of the other describing variables, $R^2_{X_i}$ will be large, close to 1.0. Consequently $1/(1 - R^2_{X_i})$ and the variance of $\hat{\beta}_i$ will grow larger as $R^2_{X_i}$ approaches 1.0. And so the estimate of $\hat{\beta}_i$ grows more insecure as $R^2_{X_i}$ approaches closer to 1.0.

Although multicollinearity is sometimes viewed as a problem of the intercorrelation of two describing variables, it can be seen here that the variances of the estimated regression coefficients will be big *whenever* $R^2_{X_i}$ is large—which can result from a high intercorrelation between two of the describing variables *or* from a combination of three or more of the describing variables accurately predicting another describing variable. Note the variance of $\hat{\beta}_i$ is infinite when $R^2_{X_i}$ is unity (that is, when a describing variable X_i is perfectly predicted by one or more of the other describing variables). In this case, of course, it is literally impossible to tell X_i from another describing variable or combination of other describing variables. The equation for the variance of $\hat{\beta}_i$ also shows that the variance of the estimates of the regression coefficients will decrease as additional data are collected (as N grows larger).

In summary, the symptoms of multicollinearity in regression analysis include:

1. high intercorrelations between the describing variables,
2. large variances in the estimates of the regression coefficients,
3. large $R^2_{X_i}$,
4. large R^2_Y coupled with statistically nonsignificant regression coefficients,
5. large changes in the values of estimated regression coefficients when new variables are added to the regression, and
6. inability of computer program to compute regression coefficients because of inability to compute the inverse of the correlation matrix (which occurs only in very severe cases of multicollinearity—in most cases the estimation procedures produce numbers as usual).

Cures for multicollinearity can sometimes be found in the following list:

1. Collect additional data, concentrating on gathering information that will alleviate the difficulty. In some research contexts, this may involve seeking information on deviant cases or special combinations of the describing variables. Johnston cites an econometric example: "Early demand studies, for example, which were based on time-series data, often ran into difficulties because of the correlation between the explanatory variables, income and prices, plus the often inadequate variation in the income series. The use of cross-section budget data, however, gives a wide range of income variation, thus permitting a fairly precise determination of the income coefficient, which can then be employed in the time-series analysis."[8]

2. Give up on nonexperimental data and consider research designs in which the key variables can be systematically varied or at least randomized out. Do experiments.

3. Remove some of the variables from the regression that are causing the trouble. For example, if two of the describing variables are highly correlated, compute regressions with only one of the variables present at a time. Or combine the variables into a summary measure (less often an approved strategy). These steps should be taken only if they make good substantive sense.

Although the use of additional information and special statistical techniques may at times alleviate the problem, it often happens in social research based on "experiments" performed by nature that it will be difficult to obtain the independent variation necessary to assess the independent effects of the describing variables. Thus some theories that assert the importance of one variable over another, while theoretically testable, are actually incapable of being tested in the face of multicollinearity.

Finally, it is important to be clear about the signs of multicollinearity and just when it is a genuine threat to the validity of a study. It is not a sound or a fair statistical criticism to cry "multicollinearity" to discredit every analysis involving three or more variables.

A multicollinearity problem arose in the report on *Equality of Educational Opportunity* by James Coleman and others.[9] The model used seeks to explain student achievement in school (as measured

[8] J. Johnson, *Econometric Methods*, 2d ed. (New York: McGraw-Hill, 1972), p. 164.

[9] James Coleman, Ernest Q. Campbell, Carol J. Hobson, James McPartland, Alexander M. Mood, Frederic Weinfield, and Robert L. York, *Equality of Educational Opportunity* (Washington, D.C.: Office of Education, 1966). Parts of the report are reprinted in E. R. Tufte, ed., *The Quantitative Analysis of Social Problems* (Reading,

by test scores) with two clusters of variables, measures of family background aiding children in their schoolwork (such as books in the home) and measures of school resources such as the teacher-student ratio and the number of books per student in the library. In compressed form, the model is:

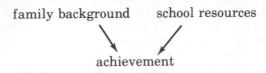

family background   school resources

achievement

The analysis proceeded by first regressing achievement against the family background variables, which yielded an R^2. Then a new regression was computed that included the school resources variables as well as family background, yielding a coefficient of R'^2. The difference,

$$R'^2 - R^2,$$

was taken as measure of the effect of school resources on educational achievement. Although using the increase in the percent of variance explained as a measure of school resource effects on education did not ultimately compromise the main findings of the study, the method would tend to underestimate school effects somewhat and received criticism. Bowles and Levin wrote:

> The most severe deficiency of the regression analysis is produced by the addition to the proportion of variance in achievement scores explained (addition to R^2) by each variable entered in the relationship as a measure of the *unique* importance of that variable. For example, assume that we seek to estimate the relationship between achievement level, Q, and two explanatory variables, X_1 and X_2. The approach adopted in the Report is to first determine the amount of variance in Q that can be statistically explained by one variable, say X_1, and then to determine the amount of variation in Q that can be explained by both X_1 and X_2. The increment in explained variance (i.e., the change in the coefficient of determination, R^2) associated with the addition of X_2 to the explanatory equation is the measure used in the Report for the unique effect of that variable on Q. Thus, if X_1 explained 30 percent of the variance in Q and X_1 and X_2 together explained 40 percent, the difference, or 10 percent, is the measure of the unique effect of X_2.

Mass.: Addison-Wesley, 1970), 285–351. See also Frederick Mosteller and Daniel P. Moynihan, eds., *On Equality of Educational Opportunity* (New York: Random House, 1972).

If X_1 and X_2 are completely independent of each other (orthogonal), the use of addition to the proportion of variance explained as a measure of the unique explanatory value of X_1 and X_2 is not objectionable. X_1 will yield the same increment to explained variance whether it is entered into the relationship first or second, and vice versa. But when the explanatory variables X_1 and X_2 are highly correlated with each other, as are the background characteristics of students and the characteristics of the schools that they attend, the addition to the proportion of variance in achievement that each will explain is dependent on the order in which each is entered into the regression equation. By being related to each other, X_1 and X_2 share a certain amount of explanatory power which is common to both of them. The shared portion of variance in achievement which could be accounted for by either X_1 or X_2 will always be attributed to that variable which is entered into the regression first. Accordingly, the explanatory value of the first variable will be overstated and that of the second variable understated.

The relevance of this problem to the analysis in the Report is readily apparent. The family background characteristics of a set of students determine not only the advantages with which they come to school; they also are associated closely with the amount and quality of resources which are invested in the schools. As a result, higher status children have two distinct advantages over lower status ones: First, the combination of material advantages and strong educational interests provided by their parents stimulate high achievement and education motivation; and second, their parents' relatively high incomes and interest in education leads to stronger financial support for and greater participation in the schools that their children attend. This reinforcing effect of family background on student achievement, both directly through the child and indirectly through the school, leads to a high statistical correlation between family background and school resources.

The two sets of explanatory variables are so highly correlated that after including one set in a regression on achievement, the addition to the fraction of total variance explained (R^2) by the second set will seriously understate the strength of the relationship between the second variables and achievement. Yet the survey made the arbitrary choice of first "controlling" for student background and then introducing school resources into the analysis. Because the student background variables—even though crudely measured— served to some extent as statistical proxies for school resources, the later introduction of the school resource variables themselves had a small explanatory effect. The explanatory power shared jointly by school resources and social background was thus associated entirely with social background. Accordingly, the importance of background factors in accounting for differences in achievement is systematically inflated and the role of school resources is consistently underestimated.[10]

[10] Samuel Bowles and Harry Levin, "The Determinants of Scholastic Achievement—An Appraisal of Some Recent Evidence," *Journal of Human Resources*, 3 (© 1968 by the Regents of the University of Wisconsin), pp. 14–16.

Example 3: A Five-Variable Regression—
The Size of Democratic Parliament

Here we examine a five-variable multiple regression that illustrates
the following statistical points:

- taking logarithms to test a "cube root law" by converting the
  law into a linear model,
- interpreting a regression coefficient as an elasticity,
- using R_i^2 as a check for multicollinearity,
- using a "dummy variable" so that a dichotomous, categoric variable
  can be included in a regression,
- interpreting R^2 as the square of the correlation between the
  observed and predicted values of the response variable.

The multiple regression reported here evaluates some of factors
determining parlimentary size—the number of representatives in the
lower house—in twenty-nine relatively democratic countries of the
world. Parliaments differ greatly in size; Liechstenstein's Diet has
15 deputies, the Italian Chamber of Deputies has 630 members, West
Germany's Bundestag 496, the French National Assembly 481, and
Sweden's new unicameral parliament 350. Some large countries have
relatively small parliments: India, with a population $2^{1}/_2$ times that
of the United States, has 500 deputies sitting in its House of the
People with each deputy representing, on average, over one million
citizens. At the other extreme, the 19,000 residents of San Marino
have a 60-member Great and General Council—resulting in one
representative for every 320 citizens.

The number of representatives elected to parliament determines,
in part, the extent to which local interests are represented at the
national level; larger parliaments, other things (especially population)
being equal, permit a more precise representation. However, in larger
parliaments each member not only has an arithmetically smaller voice,
but also larger parliaments typically have greater centralization of
leadership and more rules limiting the conduct of their members
both in debate and in the diversity of their concerns. These two
conflicting factors—the representation of citizens and the manage-
ability of the chamber—must be resolved by the framers of new
constitutions. Many constitutions of the eighteenth and nineteenth
centuries specified a particular ratio of citizens to representatives,
and parliamentary size grew right along with the population.

As a consequence of this mixture of factors, parliamentary size is closely linked to population: the more populous countries have larger

$$\text{number of members of parliament} = (\text{population})^{1/3}.$$

Dodd correlated these variables and found that the cube root of population explained 67 percent of the variation in parliamentary size for 55 nations in 1950.

Dodd's model may be written by taking logarithms

$$\log \text{ members} = 1/3 \ (\log \text{ population}).$$

Thus in the regression of members (log) against population (log),

$$\log \text{ members} = \beta_1 \ (\log \text{ population}) + \beta_0,$$

the cube-root law predicts that $\beta_1 = 1/3$ and $\beta_0 = 0$. Confirming these predictions provides a better test of the law than merely correlating the cube root with the size of parliament. That correlation does not test the specific hypothesis of the law; it merely supports the general proposition that there is a relationship between the two variables. Taking the logarithms of both variables also, as we saw in Chapter 3, yields a useful interpretation of the slope of the fitted line. The estimate of the slope, β_1, measures the *percentage change* in the size of parliament associated with a *change of one percent* in the size of the population: β_1 is the least-squares estimate of the elasticity of parliamentary size with respect to population.

Here Dodd's law is tested with data from twenty-nine of the more democratic countries in the world in 1970. The multiple regression in Table 4-5 shows that the population elasticity of parliamentary size is .44, indicating that if a county was one percent above the average in population size, it was typically .44 percent above the average in parliamentary size. The standard error of the estimated elasticity is quite small, .022; thus the estimate of the elasticity itself, .44, quite surely differs from the prediction of the cube-root law.

There are three other describing variables in the regression shown in Table 4-5:

Population growth rate Although many of the democracies have relatively low growth rates, there is still sufficient variability to explain differences in parliamentary size. Countries that are growing rapidly in population size tend to have smaller parliaments, other things being equal, than countries growing more slowly. When all the other describing variables in the equation are fixed at their means, a change of one percentage point in growth rate from an annual rate of one percent to two percent across countries is associated with a decrease in the size of parliament from 196 seats to 144 seats.

TABLE 4-5

Parlimentary Size (logarithm) for Twenty-nine Democracies

	Regression coefficient	Standard error	R^2_i
Population (log)	.440	.022	.14
Annual population growth rate	−.135	.020	.13
Number of political parties	.051	.013	.26
Bicameral—unicameral	.066	.040	.20
$R^2 = .952$			

All coefficients are statistically significant at the .001 level, with the exception of the variable bicameral—unicameral. That coefficient is significantly different from zero at the .06 level.

Number of parties in the party system   The greater the number of parties in the present-day party system, the larger the parliament. Other things being equal, two-party systems have parliaments averaging about 137 seats; multiparty systems, 195 seats. A larger party system may reflect somewhat greater underlying diversity in the society, and the constitutional framers may then create a larger than normal parliament in an effort to represent that diversity. Perhaps a more plausible explanation is that in a multiparty system, many parties will participate in the bargaining over parliamentary size and the smaller parties will work hard for a large-sized parliament, so that at least some of their party officials will be able to hold parliamentary seats. Parliaments sufficiently large to include the leading officials of each party may be quite inflated in size, particularly if the votes of the minor parties are scattered. If such a process operated for a number of years as the distribution of seats shifted from party to party, then the incumbent parlimentarians might well favor increases in the size of parliament so that they or their colleagues would stay in office even with some shifts in the share of votes received by each party.

Bicameral—unicameral parliaments   Unicameral parliaments are typically somewhat larger than the lower chambers of bicameral parliaments. Some unicameral systems have come about from a merger of two chambers; here the interests of incumbent parliamentarians are obvious. Other things being equal, the unicameral parliaments average 189 seats in the fitted model; the lower chamber of bicameral parliaments, 163 seats.

The numerical coding for this variable was:

bicameral   = 0,

unicameral = 1.

Such a dichotomous categoric variable is called a "dummy variable," and such variables are used to include categoric variables in multiple regression models. The following are examples of dummy variables:

REGION

0 = North

1 = South

CHANGE IN A TIME SERIES

0 = before tax cut,

1 = after tax cut

SEX

0 = male,

1 = female

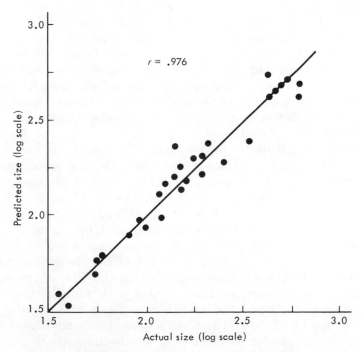

FIGURE 4-3   Actual and predicted parlimentary size, twenty-nine democracies

Table 4-5 shows the value of R_i^2, the value of R^2 resulting from the regression of the ith describing variable on all the other describing variables. The values are quite small, indicating that multicollinearity is not a problem here.

Figure 4-3 shows the relationship between the observed and predicted values of the response variable, the logarithm of parliamentary size. The correlation, $r_{Y\hat{Y}}$, between the observed and predicted values is .976. That value squared is mathematically equivalent to R^2, the proportion of variance in the logarithm of parliamentary size explained by the regression:

$$r_{Y\hat{Y}}^2 = (.976)^2 = .952 = R^2.$$

How was the regression reported in Table 4-5 chosen? At the start of the analysis, six describing variables were considered as possible candidates for inclusion in the final model. In addition to the four variables already discussed, two others were considered good candidates: whether or not the country was in Europe and the institutional age of the currently established parliament. It appeared that European countries, for one reason or another, had large parliaments. The length of time the parliament had been established under the current constitution was included as a possible describing variable on the speculation that older parliaments might be larger. Table 4-6 shows twelve different multiple regressions using various combinations of the six candidate describing variables. Let us look through these twelve different regressions to see the search for the model previously reported in Table 4-5. It will be clear that several different models could have been the model of choice.

Regression 1 is simply the two-variable regression of parliamentary size (log) against population size (log). The regression coefficient reported in Table 4-6 indicates that a change of one percent in population was associated with a change of .41 percent in parliamentary size; 76 percent of the variance was statistically explained. Regressions 2 and 3, both with two describing variables send the R^2 up to about 90 percent. Either the population growth rate or the country's geographic location in or out of Europe add an additional 14 percent to the variance explained in the first regression. This suggests that we can go much farther with a model that includes both the location and the growth rate along with population size. This is regression 4; and it doesn't work. Little additional variance is picked up—and also there is a multicollinearity problem. Note how the regression coefficients on growth and European location have shifted from their previous values in regressions 2 and 3, respectively.

TABLE 4-6

Twelve Regressions Explaining Parliamentary Size (Log)

Describing variables	Regression number											
	1	2	3	4	5	6	7	8	9	10	11	12
Population size (log)	.41	.40	.42	.41	.38	.38	.40	.39	.40	.41	.43	.44
Population growth rate		-.16		-.10		-.13	-.13	-.06		-.07	-.13	-.14
Bicameral—unicameral							.12		.11	.12		.07
Number political parties											.06	.05
European—not European			.26	.13	.20			.13	.20	.13		
Age of current parliament					.17	.13	.11	.12	.18	.13		
R^2	.760	.900	.891	.912	.916	.908	.928	.923	.934	.941	.946	.952
Number of describing variables	1	2	2	3	3	3	4	4	4	5	3	4

The numbers shown in the table are regression coefficients for each regression. Each of the twelve columns shows a different regression.

This is a sign of multicollinearity, confirmed by the correlation of −.77 (European countries have low population growth rates) between the two variables.

Regressions 5 through 9 try out various combinations of the describing variables. These trials verify the multicollinearity problem with respect to the European location variable and raise some doubts about the effectiveness of the age variable. Throwing in every variable examined so far gives regression 10, which picks up 94.1 percent of the statistical variation in parliamentary size (log) but with some problems. The European location variable is quite bothersome by now, in part because of multicollinearity but also—and more importantly— what does it mean, anyway? It is vague; such a regional variable doesn't tell us much substantively. What is it, *specifically*, about location in Europe that makes for big parliaments? So, regression 10 is about the best that can be done with the current candidate variables.

The last two multiple regressions try out a new candidate variable, the number of political parties in a country. Regression 11 reports a simple model with only three describing variables that outperforms—at least in terms of R^2—all the previous models, including those that contain more variables. It is a parsimonious model and a relatively successful one in terms of R^2. Regression 12 adds one more variable—the dummy variable on whether the parliament is unicameral or bicameral—to take the variance explained up to 95.2 percent.

What we have seen here is an empirical search through a variety of theoretically plausible models. The search started with some candidate variables, which were suggested by our political and historical understanding of what factors might affect this particular characteristic—size—of a political institution. The search was conducted with a variety of criteria for evaluating the different models that turned up: certain substantive criteria (for example, in part, the grounds for rejection of the European location variable) and certain statistical criteria (the statistical significance of individual regression coefficients, the value of R^2, and multicollinearity). Now these criteria are not "merely" statistical matters, for the statistical criteria used in the choice of the models inform us about the quantitative *quality* of the model under examination. Or, more precisely, the statistical criteria help evaluate the quantitative quality of different models within the theoretical and substantive context of the search for models. The context is vital; the best statistical techniques can't rescue theoretical models that are poor, unintelligent, or misguided.

Table 4-6 also shows one of the sad facts of building complex explanations of most political, economic, and social phenomena: often a variety of models will fit the same data relatively well. That is, the empirical evidence that is available does not always allow one to choose among different models that seek to explain the response variable. In this case, regressions 11 and 12 both do rather well; but even regressions 2 and 3 seem relatively acceptable. It is probably fair to say, however, that regressions 11 and 12 are pretty much the best among the lot. Both regressions are quite effective in predicting—and explaining—parliamentary size (log) as Table 4-5 indicated.

Table 4-6 does not, fortunately, show all possible combinations of describing variables. With six describing variables, there are a grand total of 63 different regressions involving combinations of one or more describing variables. In general, with K describing variables, there are $2^K - 1$ possible regressions. Some regression programs can, in fact, search through all possible combinations to find one or more "best" regressions. Although such searches may seem rather like brute-force empiricism (and they often are!) the criteria of choice for the best regression or regressions are intelligent and may provide a reasonable guide—when combined with substantive understanding—in searching for models. Some elegant computer programming has enabled one regression program to examine quickly every regression in cases with up to 12 describing variables—that is, 4,095 regressions.[11] The view is: If you're going to search for a model, why not search thoroughly?

Of course, we would trade all those searches in for one good idea. And that idea might come from looking at the data.

[11] Cuthbert Daniel and Fred Wood, *Fitting Equations to Data* (New York: Wiley, 1971).

Appendix

Notes On Obtaining Data And Other Information

The U.S. Government Printing Office publishes a biweekly list of recent government publications. This is free and is often quite useful for keeping up with the publication of congressional hearings. Also the GPO has many separate lists of publications by field. Write Superintendent of Documents, Government Printing Office, Washington, D.C. 20402. Note: the GPO is often very slow, with orders sometimes taking six to eight weeks to fill. Quicker access may be obtained in most large libraries (which receive most GPO documents), although this material is often uncatalogued and requires persistence to dig it out. Sometimes a trip to Washington to the GPO may be necessary. Occasionally a letter to your representative in Congress will produce quick results (and a free copy), although this method's efficiency seems to have decreased considerably in recent years. Occasionally congressional hearings may be obtained directly from the committee although such requests now tend to produce a letter referring one to the GPO rather than a free set of hearings.

Congressional hearings are a great source of information and quantitative materials in any field. The hearings consist of testimony

164

and reprints of material relevant and irrelevant to the subject at hand. Put together with a shovel, the hearings are often biased and frequently contain hundreds of pages of wacky letters, reprinted editorials, compilations of data, and other diversions. There is often no better way to get a good picture of a subject, however. For example, Morton Mintz's useful book *By Prescription Only* was substantially drawn from a long series of hearings on the drug industry. Copies of congressional hearings are generally inexpensive. Try the committee, a friend in Congress, and the GPO. There is also the *Congressional Record;* I.F. Stone's fine investigative reporting is based in part on thorough readings of the *Congressional Record* and committee hearings. It is a bit like looking for diamonds in a sewer—but there are great rewards in digging through the *Record* and through hearings.

You can usually obtain a free reprint of almost any recently published article in an academic journal by writing the author directly on a postcard requesting a copy of the article. Most academics like to send out reprints. In most journals, the author's affiliation is given: e.g.,

Samuel M. Jones

Blank University

The problem is where to find Blank University so you can write Jones for a reprint. The *World Almanac,* or *The Associated Press Almanac,* and some dictionaries list the locations of colleges and universities. There are services that provide you with a copy of the title page of all the journals so you can look through the titles and write for reprints. These are sometimes useful although your interests should be pretty serious and relatively narrow before starting in on these.

A good librarian, working in the field you are interested in, can turn up all kinds of useful things including uncatalogued fugitive materials. Some libraries even keep clipping files on various subjects. In short, a professional librarian can often provide the most thorough as well as the most efficient guide to materials.

One efficient place to start research is the *NACLA Research Methodology Guide,* published by the North American Congress on Latin America, P.O. Box 57, Cathedral Park Station, New York, New York 10025. It costs $1.00. This 72-page pamphlet lists basic research materials, journals, and addresses necessary for research of most facets of government and corporate life. It combines a radical perspective with a thoroughness in tracking down basic reference materials.

Don't forget the card catalog. Government materials are often badly catalogued and difficult to track down. Persist, looking under several possible words, and consult a librarian.

Most academic journals (and, in fact, most magazines) have student subscription rates. These rates are often very cheap and it may be more worthwhile, in fact, to take a journal as a student than later. These reduced rates tend to be disappearing with increased publication costs.

Some of the best public affairs reporting now done is found in *Science,* published weekly by the American Association for the Advancement of Science, 1515 Massachusetts Ave., NW, Washington, D.C. 20005. *Science* is a widely circulating and influential journal. Although there are many articles on physical and natural science, there is also much on public affairs. At $20 a year for 52 issues, it is a bargain. Student rates are available. Look through a few issues in the library.

A list of publications based on the 1970 census is available from the USGPO. Census data is compiled and released gradually, with priorities, some claim, set outside the Census Bureau.

Over the last few years, the reports of various presidential commissions have been distinguished both by their lack of consequences and by their first-rate research effort; commissions have perished and published. For example, the twenty or so volumes on crime, emerging from the crime commission, contain much interesting and useful data concerning crime. The commission on violence also had a distinguished publication record and there are some useful essays in the recent report of the commission on federal statistics. The research reports of the commissions are published by the GPO and the more popular reports are also published commercially in paperback.

Several different almanacs are published annually in paperback. *The American Almanac* is a paperback version of the *Statistical Abstract of the United States:* it contains 1000 pages of tables, a very good guide to data sources, and some cross-national data. Others include (in order of my preference): *Associated Press, World* and *Information Please Almanacs.*

For brief summary information and recent policial historics for the countries of the world, see *The Associated Press Almanac* and the *Political Handbook and Atlas of the World,* edited by Richard P. Amoia (Council on Foreign Relations, New York: Simon and Schuster, 1970). The latter volume, much more extensive than previous editions, provides a useful collection of political history for many countries although it interprets that history almost entirely from the point of view of its relationship to the cold war.

The United Nations produces many statistical collections; guidebooks to the literature are available.

Several handbooks of cross-national data (usually compiled by variable rather than by country, thereby permitting easy comparisons across countries on each variable) are available. One good start is Charles Lewis Taylor and Michael C. Hudson, *Handbook of Political and Social Indicators.*

AMERICAN VOTING DATA

In general, voting returns by political unit (such as ward, precinct, county, or congressional district) are available in print a year after the election and are often hard to get hold of and are usually ill-organized for analysis. Many electoral records are kept by the Secretary of State in each state and are printed in idiosyncratic state almanacs. Most state almanacs report registration rates by party for electoral subunits. For historical records, see Walter Dean Burnham, *Sources of Historical Election Data.* For recent electoral results, see a local political expert—a party official, a political scientist, or a newspaper reporter.

It is almost always the case that census tracts do not match precinct or ward boundaries—creating difficulties in matching demographic characteristics with voting patterns.

A further comment on state yearbooks: over the years, statisticians have thought a great deal about the collection, organization, and presentation of quantitative information. That activity is reflected in high standards of statistical reporting in several federal government agencies. It is true, however, that statistical reporting at the state and local level is disorganized, idiosyncratic, and often of low quality. This is particularly true for election returns published in the state yearbooks. In many cases, the data are available but simply not reported or reported in peculiar formats. Improvement in data presentation in state yearbooks might begin by a review—from a statistical point of view—of current yearbooks, leading to the development of standards of consistency and perhaps even excellence for statistical reporting. Given that state yearbook production is, in many places, rooted in local politics, it will require some political skill to encourage the adoption of new standards for the tabulation of data in the yearbooks. Walter Dean Burnham has noted an interesting side effect of the poor tabulation of elections results for most political offices in the United States: ". . . the almost incredible fragmentation of basic aggregate materials in the United States has both encouraged the preeminence of survey approaches and discouraged extensive development of aggregate-analysis capabilities." Improvement of such capabilities will provide a greater understanding of state politics, more accurate interpretations and explanations of local elections, and more widespread access to analytic material for campaign targeting in state elections. The lack of adequate statistical reporting in some states makes access to data, particularly voting and registration figures, a valuable political resource and, consequently, access has been restricted to those favored by the current incumbents.

The Research Division of the Republican National Committee has turned out useful compilations of election results following both the on- and off-year elections. The address is Research Division, Republican National Committee, 310 First Street, SE, Washington, D.C. 20003. The DNC does not seem to have produced any major research efforts.

For most political campaign purposes, finely disaggregated data (at the ward or precinct level) is more useful than more highly aggregated data (e.g., congressional districts). However, keep in mind that it may not be best to gather, for example, *all* returns for *all* major races for *all* 5000 precincts of Michigan since 1964. There are 5000 geographic precincts in Michigan and probably only about 53 actual precincts from the point of view of voter analysis. That is, adjacent precincts are often very much alike and if you know what's going on in one, you know what's going on in the other. This suggests that sampling the data or clustering the data prior to detailed collection and analysis would be valuable. For example, consider the data matrix

all elections since 1964 = 5 elections by 8
statewide races in each election by 5000 precincts.

The Democratic share of the vote for each entry would require 200,000 percentages to fill that matrix. But most of that is noninformation; it merely repeats, over and over and over, other data. There are not eight completely independent races (since the percentages vary together across the offices), there are not 5000 independent precincts, and there are probably not 5 independent elections. Cluster or sample.

Presidential and congressional voting data are, of course, more readily available than state data. For example, reliable congressional returns for all districts after the 1970 elections were easily available a mere six months after the election. Sources on presidential and congressional voting include the standard almanacs, *Congressional Quarterly* (although I have had a few bad experiences with their data), the annual *Congressional Directory* and the *Congressional District Data Book* published by the GPO. The *Congressional Directory* is strongly recommended as is everybody's favorite, *The Almanac of American Politics* edited by Michael Barone, Grant Ujifusa, and Douglas Matthew, which contains extensive data on congressional districts, including voting records, district characteristics, and political history. Be careful; there are some errors in the compilation.

The *City and County Data Book* (USGPO) contains, among many other things, the presidential vote by county. Many of the political records kept in the United States are for the 3100 counties in the United States. In general, counties are a poor unit of analysis. Often they make little political sense as units per se and little social, economic, or political life revolves around the county as a unit. Yet, in part because their boundaries have remained stable over the years, much information is collected and reported at the county level. This level of aggregation results in sometimes strange and incorrect findings solely as a result of the aggregation into counties.

Index

171